Food Equipment Digest

James Stevens
& Lois Snowberger

VNR

Van Nostrand Reinhold

ITP® A Division of International Thomson Publishing Inc.

New York • Albany • Bonn • Boston • Detroit • London • Madrid • Melbourne
Mexico City • Paris • San Francisco • Singapore • Tokyo • Toronto

Van Nostrand Reinhold staff:

Publisher: Melissa Rosati
Assistant Editor: Amy B. Shipper
Marketing Manager: Mary Fitzgerald
Senior Production Editor: Jacqueline A. Martin
Designer: Mike Suh

Production Manager: Louise Kurtz
Project Development Editor: Joan Petrokofsky
Marketing Associate: Michelle Agosta
Production Assistant: Carolyn Holfelder

Copyright © 1997 by Van Nostrand Reinhold

I(T)P® A division of International Thomson Publishing Inc.
The ITP logo is a registered trademark under license

Printed in the United States of America

For more information, contact:

Van Nostrand Reinhold
115 Fifth Avenue
New York, NY 10003

International Thomson Publishing GmbH
Königswinterer Strasse 418
53227 Bonn
Germany

International Thomson Publishing Europe
Berkshire House 168-173
High Holborn
London WCIV 7AA
England

International Thomson Publishing Asia
221 Henderson Road #05-10
Henderson Building
Singapore 0315

Thomas Nelson Australia
102 Dodds Street
South Melbourne, 3205
Victoria, Australia

International Thomson Publishing Japan
Hirakawacho Kyowa Building, 3F
2-2-1 Hirakawacho
Chiyoda-ku, 102 Tokyo
Japan

Nelson Canada
1120 Birchmount Road
Scarborough, Ontario
Canada M1K 5G4

International Thomson Editores
Seneca 53
Col. Polanco
11560 Mexico D.F. Mexico

All rights reserved. No part of this work covered by the copyright hereon may be reproduced or used in any form or by any means—graphic, electronic, or mechanical, including photocopying, recording, taping, or information storage and retrieval systems—without the written permission of the publisher.

2 3 4 5 6 7 8 9 10 PAT 01 00 99 98 97

Library of Congress Cataloging-in-Publication Data

Stevens, James, 1932–
    Food equipment digest / by James Stevens and Lois Snowberger.
      p. cm.
    ISBN 0-442-02268-9
    1. Food service—Equipment and supplies—Catalogs.
 I. Snowberger, Lois. II. Title.
TX712.S75 1996
647.95'068'2—dc20

96-23120
CIP

http://www.vnr.com
product discounts • free email newsletters
software demos • online resources
email: **info@vnr.com**
A service of I(T)P®

Contents

1	TELEPHONE AND FAX NUMBERS	1
2	HARD TO FIND ITEMS	13
3	BAKING INFORMATION	23
	Equipment and Machinery Categories	23
4	TYPICAL SHIPPING WEIGHTS	25
	Bar Area	29
5	FREIGHT CLASSIFICATION	31
6	USDA 1993 FOOD CODE—HACCP	33
	HACCP (Hazard Analysis of Critical Control Points)	33
	Bacteria Control Table	33
	Food Holding Temperature Guide	34
	Sanitation Temperature Guide	34
	Temperature Labels	34
	Thermometers	34
7	COMPUTER CATALOG AND DESIGN OVERVIEW	35
	What is First Place™?	35
8	SAMPLE SITE AND INSTALLATION PROCEDURES	45
	Correctional Facilities	45
	Healthcare	49
	Scheduling Equipment Installation	54
9	BANQUET EQUIPMENT GUIDE	55
	Selecting Equipment for a Banquet Kitchen	55

10	SANITIZING GUIDE	57
11	SAMPLE FOOD EQUIPMENT LAYOUT PLANS	59
12	SIZING A GREASE TRAP	75
	Single Fixture Installations	75
	Typical Grease Trap Chart	76
13	PLUMBING AND ELECTRIC DATA AND CONVERSIONS	77
	Gas	77
	Common Utilities Conversions	78
	Electrical Ratings	85
14	STAINLESS STEEL FABRICATION	89
	Stainless Steel Thickness and Weight	89
	Typical Gauges for Stainless Steel Fabrication	89
15	FLATWARE: SUGGESTED REQUIREMENTS	91
	Flatware: General Operations	91
	Flatware: Specific Operations	91
	Glassware: Suggested Requirements	92
	Steamtable Pan: Approximate Number of Servings per Pan	92
	Utensils: Scoop and Ladle Equivalents	93
	Soup/Sauce Ladles	94
	Utensils: Suggested Guide for Utensil Selection in Kitchen	94
16	FOOD TRADE MAGAZINES AND ASSOCIATIONS	99
	Food Trade Magazines	99
	National Foodservice Associations	100
17	VIDEO TAPES	103

Telephone and Fax Numbers

Manufacturer	Telephone	Fax	State	Zip
AM Manufacturer	800-342-6744	708-841-0975	IL	60419
Ability Metal	800-525-Hood	813-323-5963	FL	33712
Adamatic	800-526-2807	908-544-0735	NJ	07724
Admiral Craft	800-223-7750	800-447-7750	NY	11355
Advance	800-645-3166	516-242-6900	NY	11717
Aero	800-237-6634	201-473-3794	NJ	07012
Alto Shaam	800-558-8744	414-251-7067	WI	53052
AM Metalcraft	800-333-9133	800-333-6046	IL	60160
Amana	800-364-9954	319-622-5183	IA	52204
Amco Corp.	800-621-4023	312-379-5183	IL	60651
American Metal	800-333-9133	800-333-6046	IL	60160
American Panel	800-327-3015	904-245-0726	FL	34472
American Wyott	800-752-0863	307-637-8071	WY	82003
Anchor Glass	800-848-7200	800-848-0082	OH	43130
Ansul Fire	800-346-3626	715-732-3479	WI	54143
APW/Wyott	800-527-2100	214-565-0976	TX	75226
Arctic Industries	800-325-0123	305-883-4651	FL	33166
Aris Manufacturing	800-558-8565	414-481-9313	WI	53207
Atlas/Set'n'serve	800-762-7565	305-623-0475	FL	33169
Avtec	800-262-8832	708-851-5777	IL	60543

Food Equipment Digest

Manufacturer	Telephone	Fax	State	Zip
Baker's Aid	800-645-4440	800-921-4216	NY	11791
Bakers Pride	800-431-2745	914-576-0605	NY	10801
Bally Engineering	800-242-2559	215-845-6110	PA	19503
Belson Manufacturing	800-323-5664	708-897-0573	IL	60542
Berkel	800-348-0251	219-324-2928	IN	46350
Best-Value Textiles	800-732-0571	303-761-1142	CO	80150
Bettcher Inc.	800-321-8763	216-965-4900	OH	44089
Beverage Air	800-845-9800	803-582-5083	SC	29304
Bevles	800-441-1601	909-465-6020	CA	91708
Blaze Products	800-456-1017	502-633-0685	KY	40066
Blodgett Oven	800-331-5842	802-864-0183	VT	05402
Bloomfield	800-621-8556	702-345-0569	NV	89439
Bon Chef	800-331-0177	201-383-1827	NJ	07822
Booth, Inc.	800-527-7422	214-243-8075	TX	75229
Brass Smith, Inc.	800-662-9595	303-296-2320	CO	80205
Brewmatic	800-421-6860	213-234-3376	CA	90037
Bricker Products	800-733-0271	513-563-7050	OH	54241
Brown, W.A.	800-438-2316	704-637-0919	NC	28144
Buffalo China	800-828-7033	716-824-1378	NY	14240
Bunn-O-Matic	800-637-8606	217-529-6644	IL	62708
Burden China	800-822-2424	818-350-0797	CA	91732
Bus Boy	800-323-2210	800-635-4725	IL	60120
C & K Manufacturing	800-821-7795	216-871-7763	OH	44145
C.R. Manufacturing	800-328-3984	612-472-7808	MN	55364
Caddy Corp.	800-446-6129	609-467-5511	NJ	08014
Cal-Mil Plastic	800-321-9069	619-438-3959	CA	92009
Calico Industries	800-638-0828	301-498-2056	MD	20701
Cambro	800-854-7631	714-842-3430	CA	92647
Candle Corp.	800-669-6699	708-294-1111	IL	60018
Captive-Aire	800-334-9256	919-554-1227	NC	27596
Carroll Chair	800-331-4704	612-781-3433	MN	55418
Carter-Hoffman	800-323-9793	708-367-8981	IL	60060
Champion Industries	800-532-8591	910-661-1979	NC	27115
Chester-Jensen	800-685-3750	215-876-0485	PA	19016
Chicago Faucet	800-323-5060	708-298-3101	IL	60018
Chicago Metallic	800-323-3966	708-438-2175	IL	60047
Classico Chair	800-968-6655	317-472-3548	IN	46970

Manufacturer	Telephone	Fax	State	Zip
Cleveland Range	800-338-2204	216-481-3782	OH	44110
Co-Rect Products	800-328-5702	612-542-9205	MN	55427
Coldelite Corp.	800-648-4389	919-661-9895	NC	27115
Coldzone	800-772-2653	714-529-8503	CA	92621
Colson Caster	800-643-5515	800-356-6708	AR	72401
Combimaster	800-331-5842	802-865-0387	VT	05402
Component Hardware	800-526-3694	908-364-8110	NJ	08701
Comstock Castle	800-637-9188	217-223-0007	IL	62306
Connolly	800-468-4681	914-738-2186	NY	10803
Continental Refrigeration	800-523-7138	215-244-9579	PA	19020
Continental Silite	800-652-8210	403-528-6338	OK	73152
Cool Curtain	800-854-5719	714-662-0943	CA	91730
Cooper Instrument	800-835-5011	203-347-5135	CT	06455
Cornelius	800-238-3600	612-422-3226	MN	55303
Corning Foodservice	800-451-7603	708-637-1047	IL	60563
Craig Manufacturing	800-631-7936	201-923-1767	NJ	07111
Crathco	800-695-4500	507-499-0245	KY	40232
Cres-Cor	800-321-7174	216-851-9734	OH	44108
Crimsco	800-821-3912	816-444-2199	MO	64130
Crown Inc.	800-255-5678	201-672-7536	NJ	07017
Crystal Tips	800-527-7422	302-653-2065	DE	19977
CTX	800-323-5575	800-365-4725	IL	60120
Curtron Inc.	800-833-5005	518-943-9527	NY	12414
Dade Engineering	800-321-2112	305-884-6166	FL	33010
Davis Prod.	800-553-2847	219-874-4658	MI	47119
Dean Industries	800-995-1210	301-327-3343	CA	90248
Delco Tableware	800-221-9557	516-625-0859	NY	11050
Delfield	800-733-8821	800-669-0619	MI	48858
Detecto Scale	800-641-2008	516-937-0524	NY	11753
Dinex	800-523-9752	203-537-0160	CT	06415
Dito-Dean	800-331-7958	916-652-4154	CA	95677
Dormont	800-367-6668	412-733-4808	PA	15632
Douglas Machines	800-654-3382	813-449-0029	FL	34625
Duke Manufacturing	800-735-3853	314-231-5074	MO	63147
Dunhill	800-847-4206	718-625-0155	NY	11205
Duo-Aire	800-762-2473	616-388-8330	MI	49001
Dynamic Cooking	800-433-8466	714-220-9668	CA	90720

Manufacturer	Telephone	Fax	State	Zip
Econo Max Manufacturing	800-777-1507	503-667-8349	OR	97233
Elliott-Williams	800-428-9303	317-545-1977	IN	46219
Epco	800-251-1429	615-890-3196	TN	37129
Evans Refrigeration	800-346-9411	914-664-5978	NY	10553
Everpure	800-323-7873	708-654-1115	IL	60559
F.E.I. Industries	800-835-0251	401-274-3520	RI	02908
Falcon Products	800-873-3252	314-991-9227	MO	63132
Far West Products	800-545-9189	210-737-5748	TX	78201
Federal Industries	800-356-4206	608-424-3234	WI	53508
Fisher Faucets	800-421-6162	800-832-8238	CA	93275
Flame Gard, Inc.	800-334-3072	213-888-9395	CA	90040
Fleetwood	800-645-3449	215-944-9632	PA	19522
Floaire	800-326-8998	215-636-1617	PA	19020
Foldcraft/Plymold	800-533-0480	507-789-6192	MN	55946
Follett	800-523-9361	610-250-0696	PA	18044
Food Warm Equipment	800-222-4393	815-459-7989	IL	60039
Forschner	800-243-4032	800-243-4006	CT	06484
Fountainhead	800-326-8998	215-638-1617	PA	19020
Franklin Machine	800-257-7737	800-255-9866	NJ	08053
Franklin Products	800-234-2433	800-873-7757	GA	30269
Franmara, Inc.	800-423-5855	408-422-7000	CA	93902
Frymaster	800-221-4583	318-868-5987	LA	71135
Gar Products	800-424-2477	908-370-5021	NJ	08701
Garland	800-424-2411	800-624-0218	PA	18224
Gasser Chair Co.	800-323-2234	216-759-9844	OH	44505
Gaylord	800-547-9696	503-692-6048	OR	97062
Gemni Bakery Equipment	800-468-9046	215-673-3944	PA	19115
General Slicing	800-251-4232	800-221-5291	TN	37133
Giles Enterprises	800-554-4537	205-272-3561	AL	36109
Glastender, Inc.	800-748-0423	517-752-4444	MI	48604
Globe	800-34Slice	513-299-4147	OH	45401
Glolite/Nu-Dell	800-843-9211	708-803-4584	IL	60018
Glowmaster	800-272-7008	201-843-8061	NJ	07662
Gold Metal Products	800-543-0862	800-542-1496	OH	45214
Grindmaster	800-695-4500	502-499-0245	KY	40232
Groen	800-676-7332	708-439-6018	IL	60007
Grosfillex	800-523-8493	215-693-8254	PA	19551

Telephone and Fax Numbers

Manufacturer	Telephone	Fax	State	Zip
H.F. Coors China	800-782-6677	310-641-9429	CA	90301
Hall China	800-445-4255	216-385-6185	OH	43920
Hamilton Beach	800-572-3331	804-527-7174	VA	23060
Harford Systems	800-638-7620	410-272-8508	MD	21001
Hatco	800-558-0607	800-543-7521	WI	53215
Heatcraft	800-321-1881	404-723-0203	GA	30083
Henny Penny	800-543-6243	513-456-1861	OH	45320
Hobart	800-624-0208	513-339-2852	OH	45374
Hodges	800-444-0011	314-991-9227	MO	63132
Hollowick	800-367-3015	315-682-6948	NY	13104
Holman Equipment	800-225-3958	207-282-6283	ME	04072
Homer Laughlin	800-452-4462	304-387-0593	WV	26050
Hose Master	800-221-2319	216-481-7557	OH	44117
Hoshizaki	800-438-6087	404-487-1325	GA	30269
Howard Co.	800-782-6222	414-782-6515	WI	53008
Howard-McCray	800-344-8222	215-969-4890	PA	19114
Howe Furniture	800-888-4693	203-374-2287	CT	06611
Hydro Systems	800-543-7184	513-271-0160	OH	45244
Ice Craft	800-255-0626	815-624-8000	IL	61072
Idea/Medalie Division	800-833-6058	612-428-2858	MN	55374
IMC Teddy	800-221-5644	516-842-2203	NY	11726
In-Sink-Erator	800-558-5712	414-554-8917	WI	53406
Insinger Machine	800-344-4802	215-624-6966	PA	19135
Intermetro	800-433-2232	800-638-9263	PA	18705
International Storage	800-874-0375	404-787-7432	GA	30209
Jamison Door	800-532-3667	301-791-7339	MD	21741
Jarvis Casters	800-995-9876	413-283-4547	MA	01069
Jet Spray	800-538-2677	617-769-2368	MA	02062
Johnson Rose	800-456-2055	800-456-2762	NY	14095
Jordon/Fogel Refrigeration	800-523-0171	215-289-1597	PA	19137
K-Tech/Muckler	800-444-0283	314-631-7409	MO	63125
Kason Industries	800-935-2766	404-251-4854	GA	30265
Katchall Industries	800-533-6900	513-793-4230	OH	45242
Keating	800-532-8464	708-544-6505	IL	60104
Kelvinator	800-235-9157	501-450-3782	AR	72032
Kloppenberg & Co.	800-346-3246	303-789-1741	CO	80110
Kold-Draft	800-548-9392	814-455-6336	PA	15414

Manufacturer	Telephone	Fax	State	Zip
Kolpak	800-826-7036	715-425-1928	WI	54022
Krowne Metal	800-631-0442	201-485-1424	NJ	07104
L & B Industries	800-221-8752	914-354-0323	NY	10927
Lacrosse	800-345-7200	608-783-6115	WI	54650
Lakeside Manufacturing	800-558-8565	414-481-9313	WI	53207
Lambertson Inc.	800-548-3324	510-887-3154	CA	94545
Lamson & Goodnow	800-872-6564	413-625-9816	MA	01370
Lancaster Colony	800-292-7260	614-263-2857	OH	43216
Lang Manufacturing	800-426-8081	206-882-2373	WA	98073
Lawrence Metal	800-441-0019	516-666-0336	NY	11706
Le-Jo Enterprises	800-223-5356	610-296-7993	PA	19355
Leading Edge	800-327-4328	305-592-1217	FL	33122
Lee Mark Manufacturing	800-338-9886	906-863-5889	MI	49858
Leer Manufacturing	800-766-5337	608-562-3166	WI	53950
Legion Industries	800-833-9803	717-675-7551	PA	18612
Level	800-445-4337	708-888-8241	IL	60123
Liberty Woodcraft	800-448-2200	716-824-6075	NY	14127
Lockwood Manufacturing	800-521-0238	313-427-5650	MI	48150
Loren-Cook	800-289-3267	417-862-3820	MO	65803
Lucks	800-824-0696	206-872-2013	WA	98032
M & E Manufacturing	800-431-6065	914-331-4143	NY	12401
Magikitch'n	800-441-1492	215-538-3644	PA	18951
Magnuson Industries	800-435-2816	815-229-2978	IL	61125
Mainstreet Menu	800-782-6222	414-782-6515	WI	53045
Marko	800-435-0857	800-321-0857	IL	60622
Marlo Manufacturing	800-222-0450	201-423-1638	NJ	07506
Mars Air Door	800-421-1266	310-324-3030	CA	90248
Marsh Chalkboard	800-426-4244	216-343-9515	OH	44622
Mason	800-556-2766	908-469-1688	NJ	08846
Master-Bilt	800-647-1284	601-534-6049	MS	38652
McCall/Shannon	800-826-7036	715-425-1933	WI	54022
McCann's Engineering	800-423-2429	818-240-9956	CA	90039
Merco	800-547-2513	800-547-2513	OR	97402
Metal Masters	800-441-8440	302-653-2065	DE	19977
Metcraft, Inc.	800-444-9624	913-780-1155	MO	64030
Middleby	800-323-2210	708-741-9476	IL	60120
Middleby Marshall	800-323-5575	800-635-4725	IL	60121

Manufacturer	Telephone	Fax	State	Zip
Magali	800-852-5292	609-963-3604	NJ	08104
Miroil	800-523-9844	610-437-3377	PA	18105
Mirro Co.	800-558-7797	414-684-4421	WI	54221
Molded Fiber Tray	800-458-6050	814-683-4504	PA	16424
Moli-International	800-525-8468	303-777-0658	CO	80223
Moli-Tron Co.	800-525-9494	303-969-8110	CO	80228
Montague Co.	800-345-1830	510-785-3342	CA	94540
Mr. Bar-B-Q	800-333-2124	515-752-0683	NY	11804
Mueller	800-641-2830	417-831-3528	MO	65801
Multi-Flavor	800-426-8584	818-881-6734	CA	91335
Multiplex	800-325-0971	314-527-4313	MO	63021
Mundial	800-847-2224	617-762-0364	MA	02062
National Controls	800-323-2593	708-231-1377	IL	60185
Nemco	800-782-6761	419-542-6690	OH	43526
New Age	800-255-0104	913-877-3974	KS	67654
Newco Enterprises	800-325-7867	314-925-0029	MO	63303
Nexel Industries	800-245-6682	516-625-0039	NY	11050
Nor-Lake	800-955-5253	715-386-6149	WI	54016
Nordic Ware	800-328-4310	612-924-8621	MN	55416
Normandie	800-221-2398	516-944-3670	NY	11050
Nu-Vu Food Service	800-338-9886	906-863-5889	MI	49858
Old Dominion	800-245-6382	804-845-7614	VA	24505
Oliver Products	800-253-3893	616-456-7791	MI	49504
Orwak USA, Inc.	800-747-0449	612-881-8578	MN	55437
Palmer	800-444-1912	313-307-3311	MI	48036
Parvin	800-648-0770	213-585-0427	CA	90058
Pelouze Scale	800-654-8330	800-654-7330	IL	60455
Penn Refrigeration	800-233-8354	717-825-5705	PA	18702
Penn Ventilator	800-638-3267	215-934-3210	PA	19115
Perfection Equipment	800-356-6301	708-244-7205	IL	60031
Perlick	800-558-5592	414-353-7069	WI	53223
Pinnacle	800-223-3942	215-365-0024	PA	19153
Pitco	800-258-3708	603-225-8472	NH	03301
Plastech	800-538-2273	215-441-0820	PA	18974
Plastics Manufacturing	800-634-2554	214-337-7428	TX	75233
Plymold	800-533-0480	800-544-0480	MN	55946
Polar King	800-752-7178	219-426-0427	IN	46803

8 Food Equipment Digest

Manufacturer	Telephone	Fax	State	Zip
Polar Ware	800-237-3655	414-458-2205	WI	53082
Power Soak	800-444-9624	816-761-0544	KS	66062
Precision Industry	800-833-0265	305-888-2659	FL	33152
Prince Castle	800-722-7853	708-462-1460	IL	60188
Prolon	800-647-6740	601-437-3068	MS	39150
Proprocess	800-624-6717	310-869-7715	CA	90723
Pyro Chem	800-526-1079	201-335-0253	NJ	07005
Qualheim Inc.	800-348-7195	203-738-0249	CT	06057
R.F. Hunter	800-322-9565	603-742-9608	NH	03820
Raburn Equipment	800-832-2229	708-350-2657	IL	60007
Rair Systems	800-344-7247	708-940-8326	IL	60015
Randell Manufacturing Co.	800-621-8560	800-634-8369	MI	48893
Rankin	800-338-4325	213-941-7858	CA	90607
Rational	800-728-7274	708-884-9945	IL	60173
Ready Access	800-621-5045	312-376-1266	IL	60632
Reed & Barton	800-822-1824	508-822-7269	MA	02780
Regal Fixture	800-525-3692	609-261-4929	NJ	08060
Rego Corp.	800-221-1707	800-541-7615	NY	11747
Remcor	800-423-3477	708-980-8511	IL	60139
Richardson Seat	800-522-1883	312-829-8337	IL	60612
Richlite	800-445-3416	800-635-0542	WA	98119
Robertson Furniture	800-241-0713	706-886-8998	GA	30577
Robot Coupe	800-824-1646	601-956-5758	MS	39206
Royal Industries	800-782-1200	800-321-3295	IL	60622
Royal Paper Products	800-666-6655	215-384-3400	PA	19320
Royalton Foodservice	800-662-8765	216-237-1694	OH	44133
Rubbermaid	800-347-9800	800-331-3291	VA	22601
Russell Harrington	800-524-0770	508-764-2897	MA	01550
Sage Systems	800-423-0150	805-527-7661	CA	93065
Salvajor	800-821-3136	800-832-9373	MO	64132
Sanjamar	800-248-9826	414-723-4204	WI	53121
Sani-Top	800-874-6094	904-985-0202	FL	32130
Sanwa Cutlery	800-821-7849	816-931-3272	MO	64141
Savory Equipment	800-526-2381	908-364-1518	NJ	08701
Scotsman Ice Systems	800-726-8762	708-913-9844	IL	60061
Seco	800-544-3057	314-239-7859	MO	63090
Sedgwick	800-648-1589	704-283-7135	NC	28111

Manufacturer	Telephone	Fax	State	Zip
Sensor Products	800-468-3663	313-533-5475	IL	60624
Servend	800-367-4233	812-246-9922	IN	47172
Server Products	800-558-8722	414-251-2688	WI	53052
Service Ideas	800-328-4493	612-333-6770	MN	55402
Servolift/Eastern	800-727-3786	617-825-1292	MA	02125
Shannon Group	800-826-7036	715-425-1933	WI	54022
Ship'n Out	800-431-8242	915-278-6472	NY	10509
Sico	800-533-7426	612-941-6688	MN	55439
Signets	800-775-6368	216-946-4646	OH	44060
Signologies	800-637-8639	800-336-6118	NH	03874
Silite	800-654-8210	405-528-6338	OK	73152
Silver King	800-328-3329	612-553-1209	MN	55441
Sims Seating	800-729-8178	404-954-1935	GA	30248
Sitco	800-531-5767	800-535-4235	GA	30075
Smokaroma	800-331-5565	918-667-3935	OK	74829
Snap-Drape, Inc.	800-527-5147	214-233-1330	TX	75006
Southbend	800-348-2558	919-552-9798	NC	27526
Southern Equipment	800-878-0660	315-481-8170	MO	63116
Southern Pride	800-851-8180	618-993-5960	IL	62959
Sparta Brush	800-356-8366	608-269-3293	WI	54656
Spill-Stop	800-323-0722	708-345-4067	IL	60160
Spray Master	800-548-3373	501-636-3245	AR	72756
Stainless Fabricating	800-525-8966	303-733-5863	CO	80223
Stainless Inc.	800-877-5177	305-421-4464	FL	33441
Standard Keil	800-221-0704	908-449-8767	NJ	08720
Stanley Knight	800-253-9870	616-426-4448	MI	49119
Star Manufacturing	800-264-7827	314-994-0406	MO	63132
Stephen Machinery	800-783-7428	614-771-0269	OH	43228
Stero	800-762-7600	707-762-5036	CA	94954
Stoelting, Inc.	800-558-5807	800-545-0662	WI	53042
Stratford Control	800-548-4125	203-386-1350	CT	06601
Super Chef	800-231-3478	713-729-8404	TX	77085
Super Systems	800-558-5880	414-437-9274	WI	54308
Super Sturdy	800-253-4833	919-536-2118	NC	27890
Supremetal Inc.	800-645-2526	404-740-6010	GA	30201
Syracuse China	800-448-5711	315-455-6763	NY	13221
T & S Brass	800-476-4103	803-834-3518	SC	29690

Food Equipment Digest

Manufacturer	Telephone	Fax	State	Zip
Tabco	800-645-3166	214-932-4795	TX	75142
Tablecraft	800-323-8321	708-855-9012	IL	60031
Tableskirting	800-458-8633	713-723-8627	TX	77035
Tara Linens	800-476-8272	919-774-3525	NC	27331
Taylor Co.	800-255-0626	815-624-8000	IL	61072
Teknor Apex	800-556-3864	401-725-8095	RI	02861
Therma-Systems	800-526-7673	908-561-1123	NJ	07080
Therma-Stor	800-533-7533	608-222-1447	WI	53708
Thermal Bags	800-622-5560	708-741-2288	IL	60123
Thermo-Kool	800-647-7074	601-649-0558	MS	39441
Thermodyne	800-526-9182	219-426-0427	IN	46803
Thonet	800-551-6702	704-873-6124	NC	28677
Titan	800-323-2210	800-635-4725	IL	60120
Toastmaster	800-323-2210	800-635-4725	IL	60120
Toastwell Co.	800-633-2608	314-371-2700	MO	63110
Toppo Manufacturing	800-648-1849	702-331-2730	NV	89431
Town Food Service	800-221-5032	212-460-9428	NY	10003
Tradeco International	800-628-3738	708-628-6616	IL	60101
Traex	800-356-8006	608-849-2579	WI	53529
Trak-Air, Inc.	800-688-8725	303-694-3575	CO	80112
Traulsen	800-825-8220	718-961-1390	NY	11356
Tru Hone Corp.	800-237-4663	904-622-9180	FL	34470
True Food Service Equipment	800-325-6152	314-272-2408	MO	63366
Tu-Way American	800-537-3750	800-426-3964	OH	45882
Uniflow	800-548-9392	814-455-6336	PA	16514
Union Steel	800-543-5193	517-629-9009	MI	49224
United Show Case	800-526-6382	201-438-2630	NJ	07075
Univex	800-258-6358	800-356-5614	NH	03079
U.S. Range	800-995-1210	310-327-3343	CA	90248
Useco	800-251-3398	615-890-3196	TN	37129
Varimixer	800-222-1138	318-868-5987	LA	71106
Ventmark	800-331-5582	317-843-0819	IN	46032
Vent Master	800-392-2733	713-373-5039	TX	77429
Victory Refrigeration	800-523-5008	609-428-7299	NJ	08003
Virco	800-448-4726	501-450-1142	CA	90501
Vita Mix Corp.	800-848-2649	216-235-3726	OH	44138
Vitro Seating	800-325-7093	314-241-8723	MO	63147

Manufacturer	Telephone	Fax	State	Zip
Vollrath	800-558-7631	414-459-6570	WI	53082
Vulcan-Hart	800-999-9815	800-333-1808	KY	40201
Walco Stainless	800-879-2526	315-733-6602	NY	13503
Walsh & Simmons	800-727-0364	314-664-0703	MO	63104
Waring	800-4-Waring	203-738-0249	CT	06057
Wasserstrom	800-444-4697	614-443-6499	OH	43207
Waste King	800-669-8925	213-588-8516	CA	90040
Waymar	800-328-4299	800-367-1366	MN	55337
Weavewood Inc.	800-367-6460	612-544-3137	MN	55426
Welbilt Corp.	800-222-1138	203-325-9800	CT	06905
Wells Manufacturing	800-777-0450	800-356-5142	NV	89439
West Bend	800-558-1785	414-334-6800	WI	53095
White Mop	800-237-7582	813-971-6090	FL	33617
White Mountain	800-343-0065	508-297-0044	MA	01475
Wilbur Curtis Co.	800-421-6150	213-269-3288	CA	90063
Will & Baumer	800-733-7337	315-451-0120	NY	13221
Wilshire Corp.	800-872-2526	404-263-7380	GA	30092
Wilton Armetale	800-826-0088	717-653-6573	PA	17752
Win-Holt	800-444-3595	516-222-6529	NY	11530
Wisco Industries	800-999-4726	608-835-7399	WI	53575
Wittco Foodservice Equipment	800-367-8413	414-354-2821	WI	53223
Wolf Range	800-366-9653	310-637-7931	CA	90224
World Dryer Corp.	800-323-0701	708-449-6958	IL	60163
World Tableware	800-937-3675	800-283-4959	CT	06492
Yorkraft	800-872-2044	717-846-3213	PA	17405
Zephyp Manufacturing	800-821-7197	816-827-0713	MO	65302
Zeroll	800-872-5000	407-461-1061	FL	34954

Helpful Tips:
800 and fax numbers are listed for quick reference. The manufacturer's state is listed so you can determine whether the manufacturer is open for business at a given time of day from your time zone. Also, by knowing the state, you can closely estimate the number of days required for shipping. Use the zip code and the information listed in Typical Shipping Weights (page 25) and Freight Classification (page 31) to determine approximate freight cost.

2

Hard to Find Items

Air Cleaners

Honeywell, Inc.	800-345-6770	MN	55422
Smokeeter	800-543-1300	OH	45242
United Air Specialists	800-543-1300	OH	45242

Air Curtains for Entrance Ways

Berner	800-245-4455	PA	16105
Loren Cook	417-869-6474	MO	65803
Mars	800-421-1266	CA	90248

Awnings and Canopies

Anchor Industries	812-867-4637	IN	47711
Awningtec Inc.	519-743-7599	Canada	N2B 2E1
City Awning	212-289-9266	IN	46613
E-Z Up	909-466-8333	Canada	91764
Federal Sign	708-575-2500	IL	60521
Food Court Facades	404-880-4690	GA	30303
Grate Signs, Inc.	815-729-9700	IL	60436
IFAI-Awning Division	612-222-2508	MN	55101
Lil Orbits, Inc.	612-559-7505	MN	55447
Moseley Corp.	508-520-4004	MA	02038
Universal Sign	813-855-5400	FL	34677

Bagel Slicer
Oliver Products Co. ....800-253-3893...............MI...............49504

Banner Mounting
Security Lighting ....800-544-4848...............IL...............60645

Blackboards, Neon
Neon Blackboard ....800-322-Sign...............MN...............55416

Books, Food Service
Van Nostrand Reinhold ....212-254-3232...............NY...............10003

Brass Fittings, Tubing
Brass Smith ....303-296-8520...............CO...............80205
Crown Industries ....201-672-2277...............NJ...............07017
Flitz International ....414-534-5896...............WI...............53185

Bulletin Boards
Glolite ....708-803-4500...............IL...............60018
International Patterns ....516-667-9400...............NY...............11729

Cash Drawers
Indiana Cash Drawer ....800-227-4379...............IN...............46176

Casters
Franklin Machine ....404-631-0990...............GA...............30269
Haynes Manufacturing ....216-631-2166...............OH...............44113
Jarvis & Jarvis ....800-995-9876...............MA...............01069
Win-Holt Equipment ....516-222-0335...............NY...............11590

Chinese-style Equipment
TFSE, Co. ....212-423-8355...............NY...............10003

Coat and Hat Checking
Gaychrome ....708-639-3900...............IL...............60013

Coffee Grinders
Bunn-O-Matic ....217-529-6601...............IL...............62708
Faema ....203-334-7100...............CT...............06430
Grimac Royal ....516-689-2235...............NY...............11733
Grindmaster ....800-626-6371...............KT...............40299

Hard to Find Items

Coin Sorters
LAI .... 714-373-2993 .... CA 92641

Condiment Containers/Holders
American Can Company .... 203-552-2000 .... CT 06830

Conversions, Portable Field
Rainbow Products .... 517-482-5363 .... MI 48912

Cooling-Freezing Tunnel, Accelerated Freeze Systems
Enersyst .... 214-357-9191 .... TX 75220

Cork Screws, Commercial
Franmara .... 800-423-5855 .... CA 91313

Cotton Candy Machines
C. Cretors & Co. .... 312-588-1690 .... IL 60618
Gold Metal Products .... 513-381-1313 .... OH 45214

Crepe Machines
Lil Orbits, Inc. .... 612-559-7505 .... MN 55447
Silesia .... 813-544-1340 .... FL 33709

Dance Floors, Portable
Crown Industries .... 201-672-2277 .... NJ 07017
Event .... 708-352-3642 .... IL 60525
King Arthur .... 704-872-0300 .... NC 28677
Midwest Folding Products .... 800-621-4716 .... IL 60608
Sico Inc. .... 612-941-1700 .... MN 55440
Stageright Corp. .... 800-438-4499 .... MI 48617
Wenger Corp. .... 507-451-3010 .... MN 55060

Delimers—Coffee Urns, Steam Cookers
Butler Engineering .... 201-688-3300 .... NJ 07205

Dispensers, Straws, Cones, Paper Cups
Diversified Products .... 312-772-6400 .... IL 60639
Rite Cup .... 708-455-9030 .... IL 60131
Tomlison Industries .... 216-586-3400 .... OH 44125
Traex .... 608-849-2500 .... WI 53529

Display Foods, Authentic Replica
Fax Foods, Inc. ....800-929-1189...............MO 64850

Doors
Eliason Corp.......................................800-828-3655...............MI 49003

Drive-Thru Wireless Audio System
HME..619-535-6060...............CA...............92121

Dumbwaiters
Sedgewick Lifts..................................800-431-8252...............NY 12602

Egg Mixer & Separator
Egg King ....717-731-5780...............CA...............92680

Electronic Video Games
Fun Industries ....309-755-5021...............IL 61244
NTN..619-438-7400...............CA...............92009

Fibra Ment (baking stone, pizza)
Awmco, Inc. ....312-846-1760...............IL 60620

Filters (water) for Beverage Systems
Crystal Tips ....800-441-8440...............TX...............75006
Everpure ....312-654-4000...............IL 60559
IMI Cornelius ....612-421-6120...............MN............55303
Ice-O-Matic.......................................303-371-3737...............CO..............80239
Manitowoc ....414-682-0161...............WI..............54220
Multiplex...314-256-7777...............MO............63021

First Aid Equipment
Benchmark ....708-425-4764...............IL 60453

Flatware Retrievers, Magnetic
Katchall Industries..............................800-533-6900...............OH 45242

Floor Drains, Food Service
Zurn Industries...................................814-455-0921...............PA 16514

Flowers, Foliage, Plants
Forever Fresh ....305-742-3888...............FL 33319

Green Street Co. .... 206-486-3705 .... WA 98072
Hollowick, Inc. .... 315-682-2163 .... NY 13104
Micky's Mini's .... 314-849-1127 .... MO 63127

Folding Doors, Commercial
Kwik-Wall .... 217-522-5553 .... IL 60708

Foodservice Systems
Cryovac .... 800-845-3456 .... SC 29334

Grating, Stainless Steel (entrance, grills, trenches, drains)
Kadee .... 800-321-3827 .... OH 44139

Greenhouses
Four Seasons .... 800-FOUR-SEASONS .... NY 11735

Hand Dryers
American Hotel Register .... 708-564-4000 .... IL 60062
Krups .... 312-751-9175 .... IL 60610
Royal Industries .... 312-733-4920 .... IL 60622
World Dryer .... 708-449-6950 .... IL 60163

Hand Trucks
Nexel Industries .... 516-484-5225 .... NY 11050
Salesmaker Carts .... 800-281-2278 .... KY 40214
Win-Holt Equipment .... 516-222-0335 .... NY 11590

Handicapped Aids and Access
Access Industries .... 816-763-3100 .... MO 64030
Access Systems .... 312-649-1916 .... IL 60611
Falcon Products .... 800-873-3252 .... MO 63132
Franklin Machine Products .... 404-631-0990 .... GA 30269
Safe-Stride .... 417-886-7298 .... MO 65807
Wabash Valley .... 219-352-2168 .... IN 46982
World Dryer Corp. .... 708-449-6950 .... IL 60163

Hose Reels, Commercial
Hannay Reels .... 518-797-3791 .... NY 12193

Hotplates For Cooking
Ego Products .... 404-251-3980 .... GA 30264

Ice Bagger
Icebox Co. ....800-632-3039...............SC 29578

Ice Cream Waffle Cones
Gold Metal Products ....800-543-0862...............OH 45214
Old World Cone....................800-631-4070...............WA.............98168

Ice Handling Equipment
MGR Equipment ....516-239-3030...............NY 11696

Ice Sculpture Molds
Continental/Silite ....405-528-3011...............OK.............73152
Engineered Plastics ....919-449-4121...............NC.............27249

Information Services
Info Expediters ....404-874-7063...............GA 30377

Insect Traps
Ecolabs ....612-293-2233...............MN 55102
Frank Miller & Sons.............708-201-7200...............IL 60627
Westcoast Engineering..........714-598-2055...............CA...............91789

Islands, Eating
Eatin Island ....317-849-9555...............IN 46250

Installers, Commercial Kitchens
Nationwide Installers............201-256-1106...............NJ 07512

Kegs, Barrels, Fruit Presses
Berarducci Bros. ....412-673-0600...............PA 15132

Key and Lock Systems
Access Systems......................312-649-1916...............IL 60611
Clean Team Co......................805-581-1000...............CA...............90365
Instakey Lock ....303-761-9999...............CO.............80110
LAI...714-373-2993...............CA...............92641

Lectern, Table Top
Arthur Johnson.....................312-472-0822...............IL 60614

Lobster Tanks

Marineland Aquariums	805-529-1111	CA	93021
Midwest Tropical	708-679-6666	IL	60645
Oceanariums	904-253-9314	FL	32114

Lockers

Tennsco Corp.	800-251-8184	TN	37056

Menus/Covers

Boxer Brand	800-253-2772	MA	02127
Guest Checks	800-487-4478	CA	92138
Lexington Graphix	800-323-3910	CT	06511
Nationwide Menus	800-527-6368	WI	54601

Mesquite Wood

Cookshack Inc.	405-765-3669	OK	74601
Jacobs & Son	915-372-3298	TX	76877

Millwork

Cumberland	717-243-0063	PA	17013

Orange Juice Machines

Automatic O.J. Corp.	718-268-1492	NY	11375

Ovens, Brick

Pasquini	213-739-0480	CA	90015
Renato	214-349-5296	TX	75243
Rosito	213-937-1888	CA	90016

Ovens, Wood Burning

Bakers Pride	914-576-0200	NY	10801
Bravo Systems	818-982-7286	CA	91605
Cora Imports	708-246-2299	IL	60525
Earthstone Wood	213-656-5926	CA	90036
Hickory Industries	718-784-4613	NY	11101
J & R Manufacturing	214-285-4855	TX	75185
Ole Hickory Pits	314-334-6512	MO	63701
Pasquini	213-739-0480	CA	90015
Renato	214-349-5296	TX	75243

Southern Pride............................618-997-9348...............IL...............62959
TMR...415-621-1171...............CA...............94103

Padlock-Cooler/Freezers
School Lock Co. ....800-546-8641...............NJ...............07746

Pan Soakers (carbon removal)
Waljan Products ....714-548-6820...............CA...............92707

Partitions/Walls, Moveable
Glass & Mirror.............................313-624-5050...............MI...............48390
Hygiene-Tecknik ....905-563-4987...............Canada........L0R 1B4
Logo Skirt....................................312-521-4366...............IL...............60623
National ....800-Offices...................FL...............33014

Pastry Fillers
Ragen Systems..............................201-997-1000...............NJ...............07032

Phones, Fast Food Style
Talk-A-Phone ....312-539-1100...............IL...............08720

Recycling Equipment (can crusher, glass crusher)
C.S. Bell Co. ....419-448-0791...............OH...............44883

Refrigeration Hardware
Component Hardware..................800-526-3694...............NJ...............08701
Standard Keil...............................201-449-3700...............NJ...............08720

Rice Steamers/Cookers
Town Food Service ....800-221-5032...............NY...............10003

Safes and Vaults
Allied-Gary International..............706-554-1918...............GA...............30830
Corporate Safe.............................708-371-4200...............IL...............60658
Elsafe..415-989-6261...............CA...............94111
NKL Industries............................804-485-0200...............VA...............23323
Perma-Vault.................................215-364-0330...............PA...............19006
Security Products.........................800-1ll-Safe ....PA...............19075

Shrimp Peeling and Deveining
Jonsson-Gregor............................708-831-2030...............IL...............60035

Smokers
Cookshack .... 405-765-3669 .... OK 74601

Stages, Mobile/Folding
Metwood Manufacturing .... 717-637-5996 .... PA 17331
Midwest Folding .... 800-621-4716 .... IL 60608
Platform Magic .... 305-491-0815 .... FL 33309
Sico Inc. .... 612-941-1700 .... MN 55440
Southern Aluminum Manufacturing ..... 501-234-8660 .... AR 71753
Stageright Corp. .... 800-438-4499 .... MI 48617
Wenger Corp. .... 507-451-3010 .... MN 55060

Steam Cleaners
Sage Systems .... 800-423-0150 .... CA 93065

Steamers-Hot Towel
Inwatant USA .... 201-446-7105 .... NJ 07726

Steamers-Needle (meat and rolls)
Forenta .... 614-586-5370 .... TN 37814

Table Parts, Leveler Glides
Slideway .... 215-459-4000 .... PA 19331
Level .... 312-888-8220 .... OH 60123

Taco/Tortilla Equipment
Bakery Equipment .... 800-822-5386 .... TX 78201

Time, Recorders, Clocks, Stamps
Lathem Time .... 800-241-4990 .... GA 30378

Towel Dispensers
Bobrick .... 213-764-1000 .... CA 91605

Umbrellas, Aluminum or Outdoor
Aerovane Products .... 800-553-4417 .... FL 34229
Allibert Contract .... 704-948-0440 .... NC 28078
Contract & Leisure .... 212-206-6337 .... NY 10011
Emu .... 203-384-8573 .... CT 06606
Grosfillex .... 800-523-8493 .... PA 19551
Leisure Lite Inc. .... 305-888-7444 .... FL 33010

Lineal Group ....615-893-0300...............TN 37133
Peterson Manufacturing......................712-263-2442...............IA 51442
Syroco Inc. ....617-561-1473...............MA...............02128
Texacraft......................................800-231-9790...............TX 77274
Wabash Valley Manufacturing ....219-352-2168...............IN 46982

Uniforms and Protective Apparel
Angelica.......................................314-889-1111...............MO 63112

Vinyl Wrap Systems, Dispensers
Bulman Products ....616-363-4416...............MI...............49504

Waste Compactors
International Dynetics ....203-853-9911...............CT 06830
Jensen Champions ....305-974-6300...............FL 33310

Whipped Cream Dispenser
Gruenwald....................................508-777-0200...............MA...............01923
Rocket ....800-229-Whip...............MA...............01923
Sani Serv ....317-247-0460...............IN 46241

Wine Dispensers
Wine Keeper.................................805-963-3451...............CA...............93103

Wine Storage Equipment
Creative Environments ....215-337-7174...............PA 19406

Woks
Imperial Range ....818-357-7411...............CA...............91010
Newtech ....502-531-2860...............KY 42713
Ultra Serve...................................609-494-1231...............NJ 08008

Baking Information 3

Equipment and Machinery Categories

Flour and Ingredient Handling and Storage

Fermentation Liquid and Conventional (including dough troughs)

Mixing Equipment (including elevators and dough troughs)

Bread Make-up and Panning Equipment

Roll Make-up and Panning Equipment

Cake and Sweet Goods Specialty Equipment

Cookie, Biscuit and Cracker Equipment

Donut Equipment

Seeders, Toppers, Splitters, and Secondary Processing

Proofers and Loaders (including racks)

Ovens, Loaders and Unloaders

Depanners

Cooling and Packaging Feeding (including racks)

Pan-handling Conveyors, Stackers and Unstackers, and Storage Equipment—Washing and Cleaning

Lidders, Delidders, Lid Conveyors, and Storage Equipment

Conveyors

Slicing and Slicing Blades

Packaging

Shipping (from packing to store)

Pans, Lids and Trays

Freezers

Specialty Equipment

Environmental Equipment and Supplies

Maintenance Equipment and Supplies

Power Transmission Equipment and Controls

Sanitation Equipment and Supplies

Technical Services

Transportation Equipment

For Specific Information Contact:

B.E.M.A. (Baking Equipment Manufacturer Association)
401 N. Michigan Avenue
Chicago, IL 60611
312-644-6610 (Phone)
312-527-6640 (Fax)

4

Typical Shipping Weights

Receiving scale platform ....175 lb.

Wire shelving 72" high, 4 shelves:
    18" wire, 72" long ....120 lb.
    21" wire, 60" long ....102 lb.
    24" wire, 60" long ....108 lb.
    24" wire, 72" long ....132 lb.

Dunnage rack 24" × 48" ....24 lb.

#10 can dispenser rack, 200 can capacity ....200 lb.

Walk-in cooler/freezer, galvalume construction, without compressor, with floor:
    8' × 10' ....1400 lb.
    8' × 14' ....1800 lb.
    12' × 16' ....2660 lb.

Compressors/evaporator (low temperature):

System for remote use	**Hermetic compressors**
½ HP............257 lb.	¼ HP.............43 lb.
¾ HP............267 lb.	⅓ HP.............48 lb.
1 HP............285 lb.	½ HP.............59 lb.
1½ HP........... 418 lb.	¾ HP...........106 lb.
2 HP............498 lb.	1 HP..........112 lb.
3 HP............664 lb.	1½ HP..........140 lb.

All the following units include compressors:
    1 door upright refrigerator ....350 lb.
    2 door upright refrigerator ....550 lb.

3 door upright refrigerator .... 770 lb.
1 door sandwich unit .... 180 lb.
2 door sandwich unit .... 253 lb.
3 door sandwich unit .... 370 lb.
1 door pizza prep table .... 229 lb.
2 door pizza prep table .... 427 lb.
3 door pizza prep table .... 545 lb.
deli case 50" .... 450 lb.
deli case 74" .... 660 lb.
deli case 98" .... 880 lb.

Taco make-up table, 84" .... 550 lb.
(including compressor)

Meat choppers:
　#12 hub ½ HP .... 135 lb.
　#32 hub 3 HP .... 300 lb.

Meat saw .... 192 lb.

Mixers:
　20 qt. .... 192 lb.
　30 qt. .... 450 lb.
　60 qt. .... 700 lb.
　80 qt. .... 850 lb.

Slicer, 12" knife .... 116 lb.

Pizza dough roller-counter .... 295 lb.

Buffalo food cutter, 1 HP .... 204 lb.

Vertical cutter mixer, 30 qt. .... 340 lb.

Potato peeler, 30 lb. w/base .... 212 lb.

24" range with one oven:
　four open burners .... 334 lb.

36" range with one oven:
　grate top six burners .... 430 lb.

36" range with one convection oven .... 531 lb.

60" range with one oven and open cabinet:
　six burners and 2' griddle .... 706 lb.
　four burners and 3' griddle .... 755 lb.

60" range with two ovens:
　ten burner w/two standard ovens .... 697 lb.
　ten burner w/two convection ovens .... 820 lb.

Floor model kettles:

Electric
20 gal. ....395 lb.
40 gal. ....510 lb.
60 gal. ....640 lb.
80 gal. ....690 lb.

Gas
20 gal. ....468 lb.
40 gal. ....620 lb.
60 gal. ....950 lb.
80 gal. ....1070 lb.

Table top kettles:

Electric
10 qt. ....58 lb.
20 qt. ....140 lb.
40 qt. ....163 lb.

Gas
20 qt. ....215 lb.
40 qt. ....240 lb.

Support stand:
10 qt. ....85 lb.
20 qt. ....110 lb.

Work tables, 16 gauge stainless steel:
24" × 36" ....68 lb.
24" × 48" ....79 lb.
24" × 60" ....93 lb.
30" × 45" ....96 lb.
30" × 60" ....111 lb.
30" × 72" ....127 lb.
30" × 96" ....235 lb.

Sinks, 16 gauge, 3 compartment w/drain boards:
24" × 72" ....100 lb.
24" × 94" ....125 lb.
30" × 120" ....175 lb.

Heated holding cabinets, 23¼" wide:
32" deep, 72" high...200 lb.

Table top plastic salad bar:
4'0" ....65 lb.
5'0" ....80 lb.

Mobile buffet line:
- 30" beef cart ....300 lb.
- 30" soup cart ....250 lb.
- 30" solid top cart ....250 lb.
- 60" solid top cart ....550 lb.
- 72" solid top cart ....640 lb.
- 44" frost top ....460 lb.
- 72" frost top ....760 lb.
- 44" ice pan ....360 lb.
- 72" ice pan ....600 lb.
- 30" hot food ....265 lb.
- 44" hot food ....395 lb.
- 58" hot food ....525 lb.
- 72" hot food ....655 lb.

Plate lowerators, mobile, solid:
- 2 hole ....100 lb.
- 3 hole ....132 lb.
- 4 hole ....160 lb.

Ice cream cabinets:
- 30" × 30" ....212 lb.
- 30" × 66" ....396 lb.
- 30" × 90" ....460 lb.

Dishwashers:
- undercounter dishwasher ....175 lb.
- single tank dishwasher ....450 lb.
- 44" conveyor dishwasher ....890 lb.
- 66" conveyor dishwasher ....1250 lb.
- 76" conveyor dishwasher ....1380 lb.
- 86" conveyor dishwasher ....1650 lb.

Disposers:
- ½ HP ....45 lb.
- 1 HP ....50 lb.
- 3 HP ....115 lb.
- 5 HP ....220 lb.

Boosters, compact electric:
- 9 kW ....118 lb.
- 24 kW ....142 lb.
- 54 kW ....142 lb.

Steam table, floor model, heavy duty:
- (2) 12" × 20" openings ....100 lb.
- (3) 12" × 20" openings ....225 lb.
- (4) 12" × 20" openings ....410 lb.
- (4) 12" × 20" openings ....495 lb.

Bar Area

Glass froster:
    24" wide .... 200 lb.
    48" wide .... 285 lb.

Direct draw beer dispensers:
    2 keg .... 470 lb.
    3 keg .... 555 lb.
    4 keg .... 740 lb.

Deep well beverage coolers:
    50" .... 264 lb.
    65" .... 308 lb.
    80" .... 393 lb.
    95" .... 453 lb.

Sinks:
    5', 3-compartment .... 76 lb.
    8', 4-compartment .... 110 lb.

Chairs:
    metal, stack .... 15 lb.
    metal .... 23 lb.
    wood .... 15 lb.

Booths, 42" wide, upholstered:
    single .... 70 lb.
    double .... 125 lb.

Table bases, cast iron:
    22" square .... 21 lb.
    30" square .... 25 lb.
    24" × 30" oblong .... 27 lb.
    5" × 22" end base .... 18 lb.

Table tops, laminated:
    30" × 30" .... 28 lb.
    30" × 42" .... 40 lb.
    36" × 36" .... 41 lb.
    24" round .... 18 lb.
    36" round .... 32 lb.

5
Freight Classification

NOTE: Our classification guide is from the manufacturers and is only a guide.

The following information is required when contacting a freight carrier for a freight cost estimate.

A. Shipping point zip

B. Destination zip

C. Classification of freight

D. Total crated weight

NOTE: Inform the freight carrier if a lift gate is required for drop shipments (this service is offered by some freight carriers free of charge if advance arrangements are made.)

Equipment	Class
Booths	85
Chairs	125
Cold cabinets	200
Compartment steamers	85
Counter heat lamps	150
Counter warmers	100
Deli cases	85
Dish dollies	92.5
Dishwashers	92.5
Dishwasher boosters	85

Equipment	Class
Flat dollies	70
Fryers	77.5–85
Grills	77.5
Hoods	100
Hot cabinets	100
Mixers	85
Mobile racks	250
Ovens	70
Ranges	85
Refrigerators	85
Shelving	70
Shelves, wall	70
Sinks, 1-2-3-4 compartment	150
Slicers	77.5–100
Steam kettles	150
Steam tables	85
Tables, dining	85
Tables, work	70

USDA 1993 Food Code—HACCP

HACCP (Hazard Analysis of Critical Control Points)

HACCP is essentially a food safety assurance evaluation group that has set standards for methods to ensure that all foods produced and consumed are free of bacterial pathogens. The HACCP code is the foundation of the USDA 1993 Food Code. The standards are set up for foodservice operators as methods for checking equipment and operating practices.

The HACCP code is a check list for identifying the hazards involved in food handling and preparation. The HACCP guides provide details and specific temperature points of equipment operation and foods and identify bacterial growth ranges.

HACCP also sets standards for hygiene, food receiving and storage, packaging, and preprocessing. This includes both chemical and physical contaminants.

Bacteria Control Table

212°F	Boiling point of water.
165–212°F	Cooking temperatures destroy most bacteria. Required time to kill bacteria decreases as temperature increases.
140–165°F	Warming temperatures prevent growth but allow survival of some bacteria.
120–140°F	Some bacterial growth may occur. Large percentage of bacteria survive.
60–120°F	Incubation zone. Temperatures in this zone allow rapid growth of bacteria and production of toxins by some bacteria. Foods should move through this temperature very quickly to avoid microbial spoilage.
40–60°F	Some growth of food poisoning bacteria may occur.

32–40°F Cold temperatures permit some slow growing bacteria to cause spoilage.

0–32°F Freezing temperatures stop growth of bacteria, however, bacteria may survive.

Food Holding Temperature Guide

140°F Steam tables (minimum temperature).

30–45°F Refrigerator temperature.

0°F Frozen foods.

−20°F Frozen foods for extended time (up to one year).

Sanitation Temperature Guide

170–212°F Sanitation of dishes (minimum 170°F for 30 seconds).

140°F Wash cycle of dish machine.

120°F Hand dishwashing.

The following is a list of products on the market to assist your operators in maintaining safe food products for the consumer.

- Hand washing stations.
- Hand washing training posters.
- Sanitizers for hands.
- Sanitizers for hard surfaces.
- Antiseptic sponge: Cleans slicer blades as the sponge is cut into pieces.
- Color-coded cutting boards prevent cross-contamination.
- Color-coded brushes to avoid cross-contamination.
- Gloves, caps, and aprons.
- Surface bacteria sponges.
- Videos on food safety knowledge and training.

Temperature Labels

- Indicate product was too cold in shipment or storage (located on outside of box).
- Indicate time over the temperature. The alarm point color change indicates threshold temperature.

Thermometers

Many types of thermometers are available to indicate temperatures encountered during thawing, cooking, cooling, and storing. Thermometers are so sophisticated that they can chart temperatures, sound alarms, change the temperature at pre-set times, recalibrate, and indicate highest temperature and lowest temperature during a period of time.

7

Computer Catalog and Design Overview

What is First Place™?

First Place is a CD-ROM based master electronic catalogue for the foodservice equipment and supplies industry. You are able to browse through First Place one page at a time or search for any product, using any information that has been provided by the participating manufacturers as search criteria.

Many traditional electronic catalogues are built around the concept of fielded data, where the publishers code specific fields of data by extracting information from the product specification sheets or brochures. These publishers often make value judgments about what to include and how to categorize and link related data. This approach requires you to know how the data is structured, how it is categorized, and what values might have been captured from the product information supplied by the manufacturers.

First Place incorporates a more advanced approach to organizing data in an electronic form. Most importantly, *all* data provided by the manufacturer is available as search criteria. There is no need for you to understand how the data is organized or categorized in order to find qualifying products. You are able to view the actual text provided by the manufacturers, as well as each product brochure's pictures and drawings. Any information can be printed on a Windows-supported printer. The text can be exported to almost any word processor by selecting a menu item. Similarly, the pictures and drawings can be exported to a graphics package or a Windows-based word processor, such as Word for Windows, Ami Professional, or WordPerfect for Windows. These export capabilities facilitate production and "cut books."

First Place provides more than just product selection capabilities. You can reference each manufacturer's most current prices, list of authorized sales representatives and service and installation centers, corporate address and telephone directory, and product line overviews. Additionally, information is available from each manufacturer to highlight recent product introductions or withdrawals, engineering changes, price adjustments, and any other vital information the manufacturer wishes to convey in a timely fashion to its customers and prospects. Each buying group and trade association may also provide current information of interest to their particular audience.

For each product, information about features, freight and shipping, warranty, physical dimensions, certifications, utility connections, and optional equipment and accessories is available at the click of a button. Each page of the catalogue can be printed on a laser printer with such clarity that you will no longer a need to photocopy spec sheets.

Future enhancements will allow you to

- Fax any catalogue page directly from your computer.
- Access and extract FEDABASE compliant fielded data.
- Enter your own discounts from the manufacturer's list price.
- Maintain your own version of the Thesaurus.
- Import a list of model numbers or bar codes from another application to look-up and extract data from **First Place** or from FEDABASE.

PRODUCT BULLETIN

New Product Information from AutoMATE Systems, Neptune Beach, Florida

A Preview of AutoMATE3

AutoMATE Systems will soon ship Release 3 of it's popular AutoCAD enhancement program AutoMATEkp. Hundreds of new features and major improvements make AutoMATE3 one of the most powerful CAD environments available anywhere; and it remains the *only* CAD design tool for Food Facility Designers.

If you already use AutoMATE, you'll find many of the new features have come straight from your Wish List. New features that let you draw things you could never draw before. And features that give you more control over AutoMATE's drawing 'style' - customize the way AutoMATE works to suit your own preferences.

The feature list for AutoMATE3 is rich and long. We've added over 200 powerful new custom-fab sub-routines, added or enhanced over 400 other AutoMATE commands, and expanded the Primitives list to almost 1000 components and sub-assemblies. With Release 3, we've raised the power of AutoMATEkp to a new level - to the power of 3.

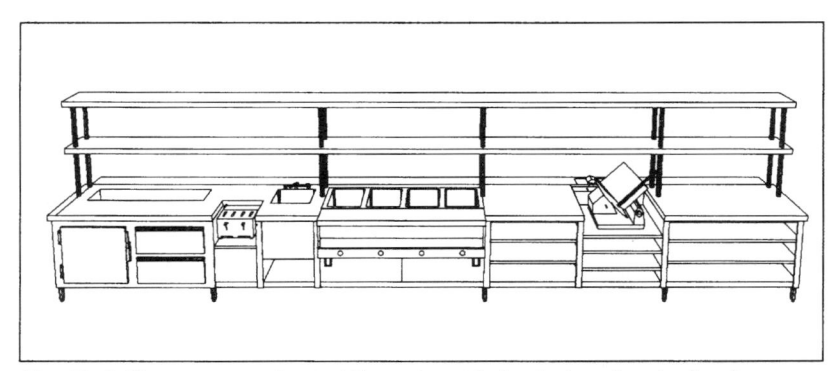

This Chef's Unit was created in just 5 minutes with the Custom Counter function.

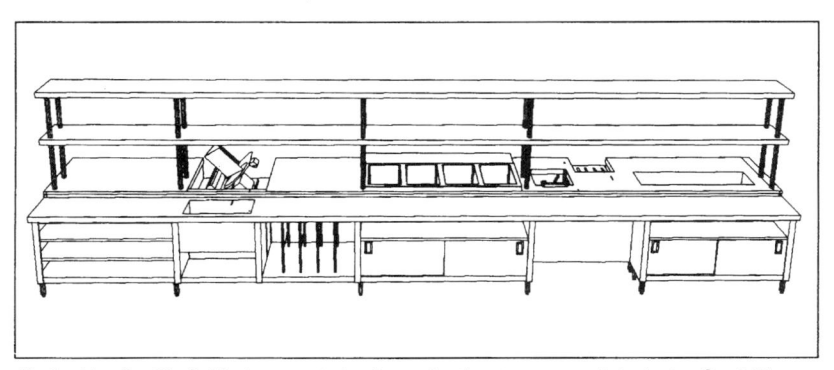

Each side of a Chef's Unit is created independently, giving complete design flexibility.

A Look Into The Future

The focus of AutoMATE Release 3 is added power, greater flexibility, and new user customization of the CAD aspects of AutoMATEkp. But we're not stopping there.

Future releases of AutoMATE will feature more user customization tools, a revamped database structure for greater flexibility, more rules-based design programs, and more front-of-the-house tools.

A Network version of AutoMATE is currently under development, and we plan to release a Windows compatible version of AutoMATE shortly after Windows 4.0 ships.

We don't have enough space here to describe all the new features in AutoMATE3, but a few of the ones we think you'll find exciting include:

Powerful FAB Commands

All fabrication routines have been rewritten to produce better 3D constructions for improved renderings and visualizations. And we've added 5 completely NEW fabrication types:

- Custom Counters
- Custom Cabinetry
- Custom Chef's Counters
- Dishtables
- Ell and U-Shaped Sinks

The new CHEF'S COUNTER command draws complex Chef's Counters in minutes, and offers a choice of three common countertop styles: Depressed Pick-up Shelf, Raised Pick-up Shelf, or a Flat Countertop.

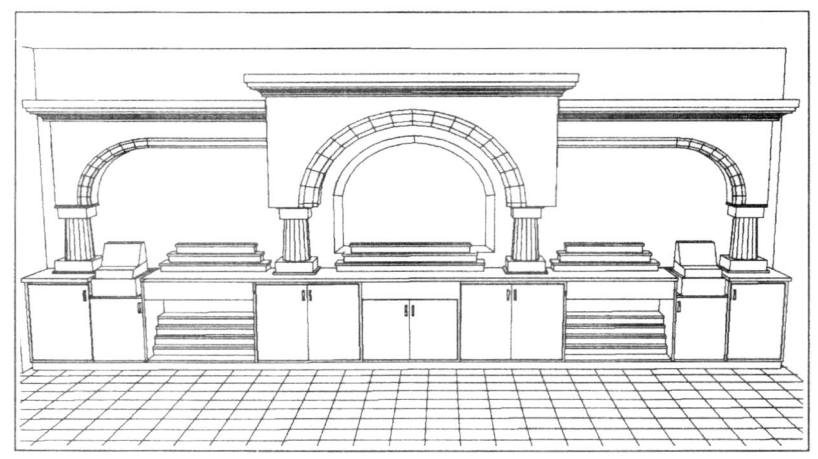

This Backbar was created with Custom Cabinetry and the 3D-SWEEP commands.

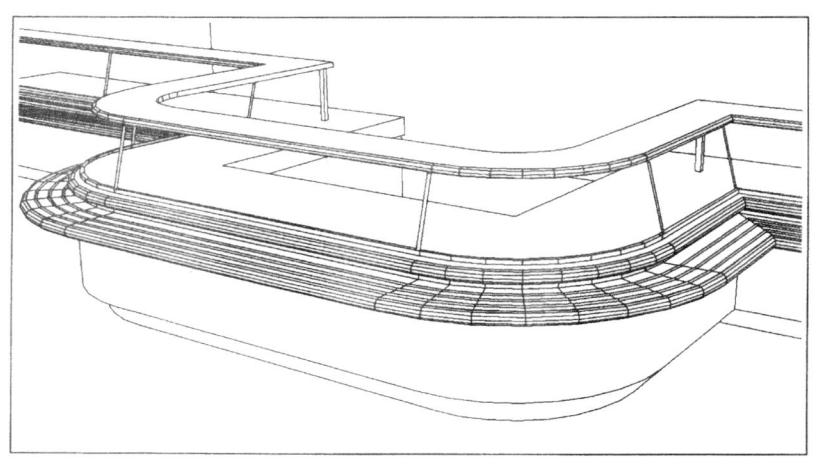

*With the enhanced KP*TILT and the new 3D-SWEEP commands you can draw just about any shape you can imagine.*

New Realistic Seating components improve front-of-the-house presentations.

The CUSTOM COUNTER function draws counters and cabinet-base tables of virtually any size and description.

The CUSTOM CABINETRY function draws typical laminate covered cabinets of many types: waitress stations, beverage stations, hostess stands, etc.

Each of the new CUSTOM FAB functions include many popular cabinet elements: Hot Wells, Cold Pans, Tray Storage, Glass Rack Storage, Single and Multiple Drawers, Refrigerated Base Sections, - over 200 different cabinet base configurations to choose from.

All Fabrication TOOLS and DETAILS commands have been enhanced adding new options and generating better 3-D for improved 3D rendering.

Multi-Purpose TOOLS

KP*Icon Tools includes two new commands that give you powerful capabilities in building new symbols of all types.

The 3D-SWEEP command "sweeps" a set of 3D-Faces thru a polyline path. With this powerful new tool, you can create sophisticated serving counters, bars and back-bars, overhead bar soffits, even decorative back-bar superstructures.

3D-FACE TRIM\STRETCH is a tool for mitering the ends of trayslides, countertops, etc. Use this function to join two straight counters into a single mitered corner counter.

Edit Inserted Symbols

Another remarkable new tool is the MODIFY ICON command. Any KP*Icon can be modified at any time in virtually any way, and then re-blocked in-place while retaining all it's intelligent characteristics.

Computer Catalog and Design Overview   39

Improved Dimensioning

AutoMATE3 Dimensioning routines now create angular as well as orthogonal dimensions. And all the Dimension routines have a built-in UNDO feature.

All Dimension routines offer a 'True Fractions' option. With this option on, dimensions are created with the more effective over/under appearance used in manual drafting.

AutoMATE3 Dimensions also now include an associative dimension technique that's even more secure than AutoCAD's built-in system.

Full METRIC Support

AutoMATE3 now has a full METRIC implementation... *all* functions have complete support for both Metric and Imperial.

All ROUGH-IN commands include a built-in UNDO feature and "rules-based" handling of the 'Common' and 'Duplicate' connection types.

And any General Purpose Utilities you add are automatically numbered and included in all Schedules and Notes.

SCHEDULES and NOTES are now completely generated from the drawing database - no more use of external text files for these functions.

Multiple Item Selection

The AutoMATE3 CadSCAN function permits selection of an unlimited number of items at once - in fact, you could select all the kitchen equipment items at one time if you'd like.

Repetitively used equipment groups can now be saved as a retrievable REFERENCE LIST, especially useful if your projects are repetitive or similar.

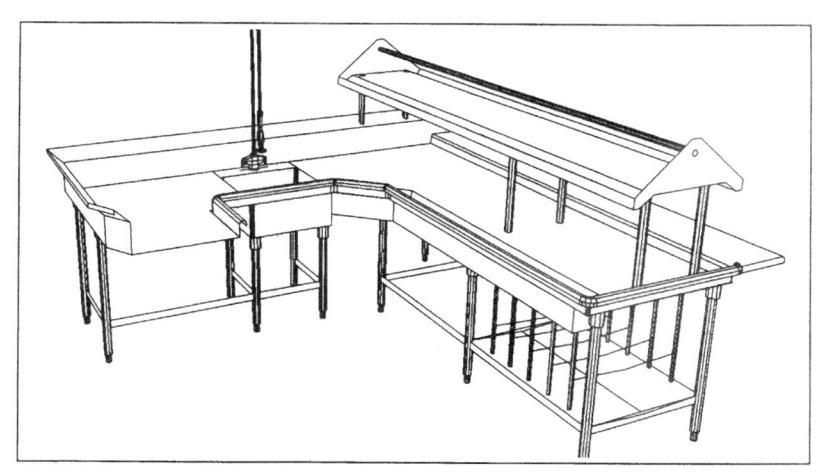

Dishtables are quickly built from the large library of typical configurations.

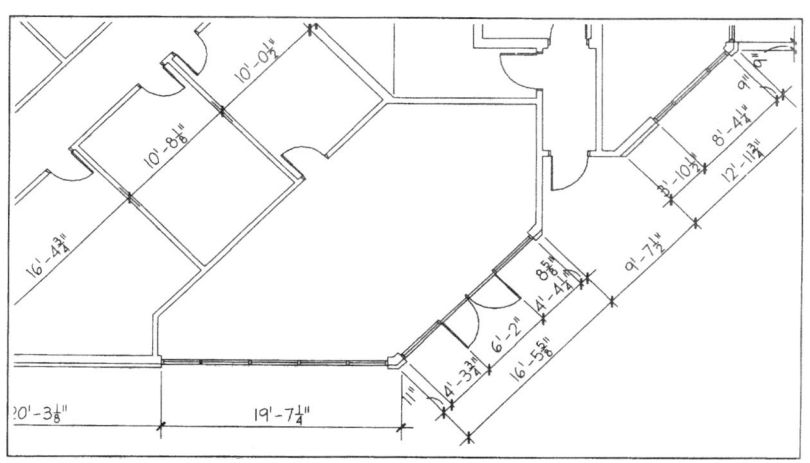

Dimension Routines handle angular as well as orthogonal walls, rough-ins, etc. The new option for True Fractions is shown here using a new simpler HAND Font.

Schedules work in Imperial or Metric regardless of how the symbol was created.

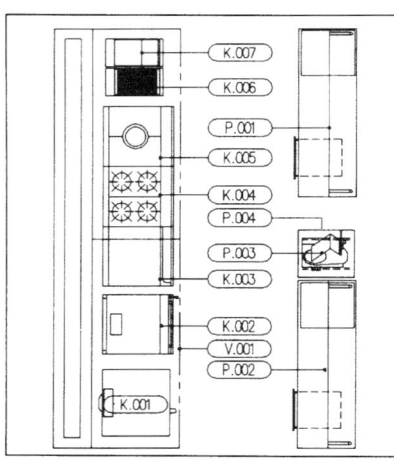

The Alpha-Numeric Style has always been on everyone's Wish List

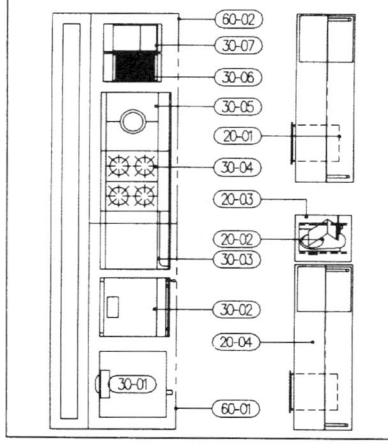

The Two-part Numeric Style is a popular way of differentiating work areas

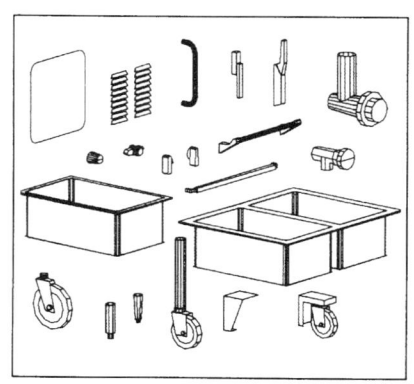

*A few of the 1000 Primitives that help you build new KP*Icons*

Pick a TAG Style

AutoMATE3's TAG command now includes a built-in UNDO feature and offers a choice of three distinct Tagging Styles.

The regular straight numeric style is still available, but has been enhanced to include *item sub-assemblies*.

The new *alpha-numeric* and *two-part numeric* styles provide greater flexibility in maintaining your drawing style.

Walls & Windows

In addition to the built-in UNDO feature, WALL commands now include a unique on-the-fly 'Reset Thickness' feature - reset the wall component thicknesses without leaving the command.

The Storefront and Multiple Panel WINDOW functions now offer a 'freestanding' option for inserting window walls between columns.

Quick Elevations

The two all-new ELEVATE commands let you create Elevation Views of a single item or a group of items in seconds. And new optimization routines can reduce the WBLOCK filesize by as much as 60%.

The GET DETAIL command retrieves any detail saved by the ELEVATE command via a screen menu selection. Your own detail drawings can also be retrieved with this function.

Creating new KP*Icons is easier than ever with a greatly expanded PRIMITIVES Library and powerful new KP*Icon Tools.

And you'll need to create fewer symbols... the AutoMATE KP*Icon format is fast becoming the new standard for foodservice equipment symbol libraries.

Easy Title Blocks

A new TITLE BLOCK Insert command takes the mystery out of adding 'smart' Title Blocks to your drawings. And your own Title Blocks can be added to the automatic insertion routine.

User Customization

AutoMATE3 includes the first of many user-customization tools that let you control how AutoMATE works. For example, you can now control:

- the default text size
- the SNAPUNIT setting
- various dimensional settings
- default Layer Groupings

For more advanced users of AutoMATE, there's new built-in support for a USER MENU and a User Lisp file. Store your own commands and utilities in your own menu file and call it from the AutoMATE3 Menu anytime you need it.

AutoMATE3... it's the most powerful food facility design tool you can use. For more information about how it can improve your productivity, please give us a call at:

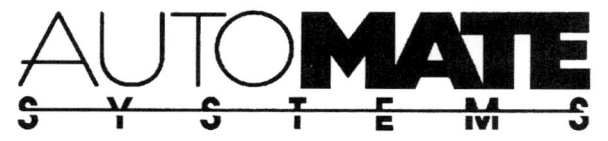

AutoMATE
SYSTEMS

241 Atlantic Blvd., Neptune Beach, Florida 32266
Telephone 904.241.3178 Fax 904.241.3177

AutoCAD is a Registered Trademark of Autodesk, Inc. AutoMATE, AutoMATE3 & AutoMATEkp are Trademarks of AutoMATE Systems. © 1994 BROCK/Associates.

Computer Catalog and Design Overview 41

Just A Few of the New Features in Auto**MATE**3

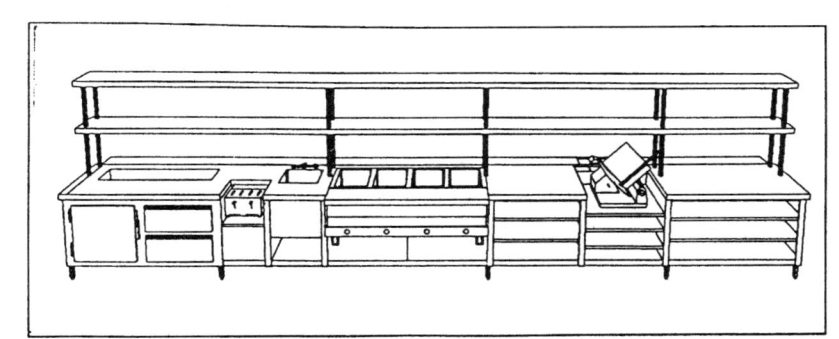

Create Complex Chef's Units In 5 minutes

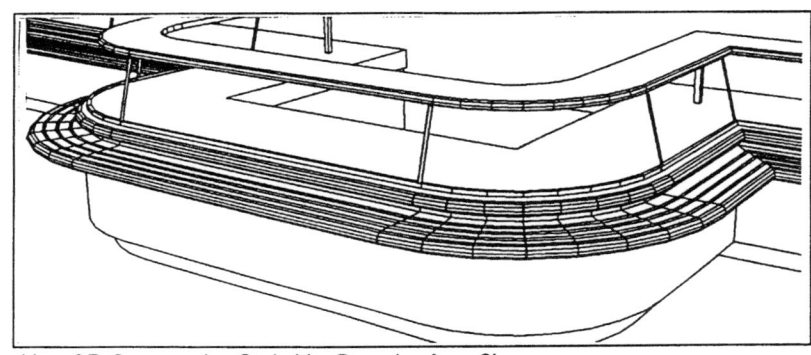

Use 3D Sweep to Quickly Create Any Shape

New Realistic 3D Furniture Enhances Presentations

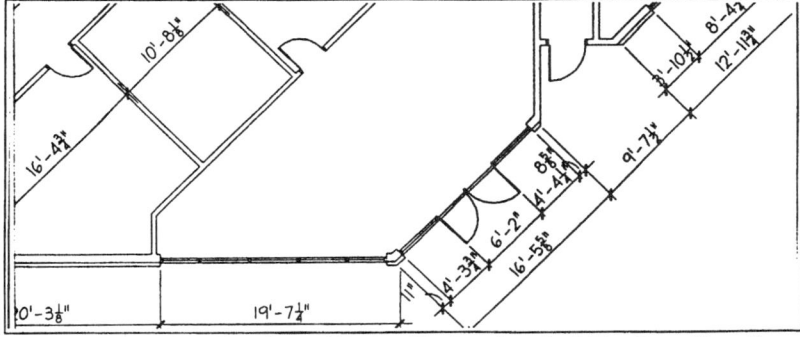

New Dimension Routines Work with Angles & Offer True-Fractions

OVER 200 NEW FABRICATION FUNCTIONS * ALMOST 1000 ICON PRIMITIVES * 'ELL' AND 'U' SHAPED DISHTABLES AND SINKS * CUSTOM CHEF'S UNITS AND COUNTERS * CUSTOM WOOD CABINETRY * SPLASH CUT-OUT FUNCTION * SWEEP A PROFILE THROUGH A POLY-LIINE PATH * IMPROVED 3-D FURNITURE * INSERT MULTIPLE SINK COMPARTMENTS * NEW ELEVATE COMMAND * TRIM AND/OR STRETCH 3D FACES TO A SELECTED LINE * MODIFY EXISTING ICONS IN-PLACE WITHOUT LOSS OF INTELLIGENT FEATURES * NEW TWO-PART NUMERIC AND ALPH-NUMERIC TAGGING ROUTINES * USE SUB-ASSEMBLIES WITH SEQUENTIAL NUMERIC TAGS * FABRICATION 'TOOLS' OFFER NEW OPTIONS * TAG AND ROUGH-IN COMMANDS INCLUDE BUILT-IN UNDO * IMPROVED UDS HANDLING IN ALL ROUGH-IN COMMANDS * ARCHITECTURAL WALL COMMANDS INCLUDE BUILT-IN UNDO * WALL COMMANDS INCLUDE ABILITY TO RE-SET WALL THICKNESS ON-THE-FLY * WINDOW COMMANDS INCLUDE DEDICATED PASS-SHELF OPTION * WINDOW WALLS AND STOREFRONTS CAN BE INSERTED IN WALL OR DRAWN FREE-STANDING * ALL DIMENSION ROUTINES NOW WORK WITH ANGULAR WALLS & ROUGH-INS * DIMENSION ROUTINES INCLUDE TRUE-FRACTIONS OPTION * EXTENDED MENU FOR SVGA * REFERENCE LISTS * MULTIPLE ITEM CAD-SCAN SELECTION * FULL METRIC SUPPORT * ETC, ETC

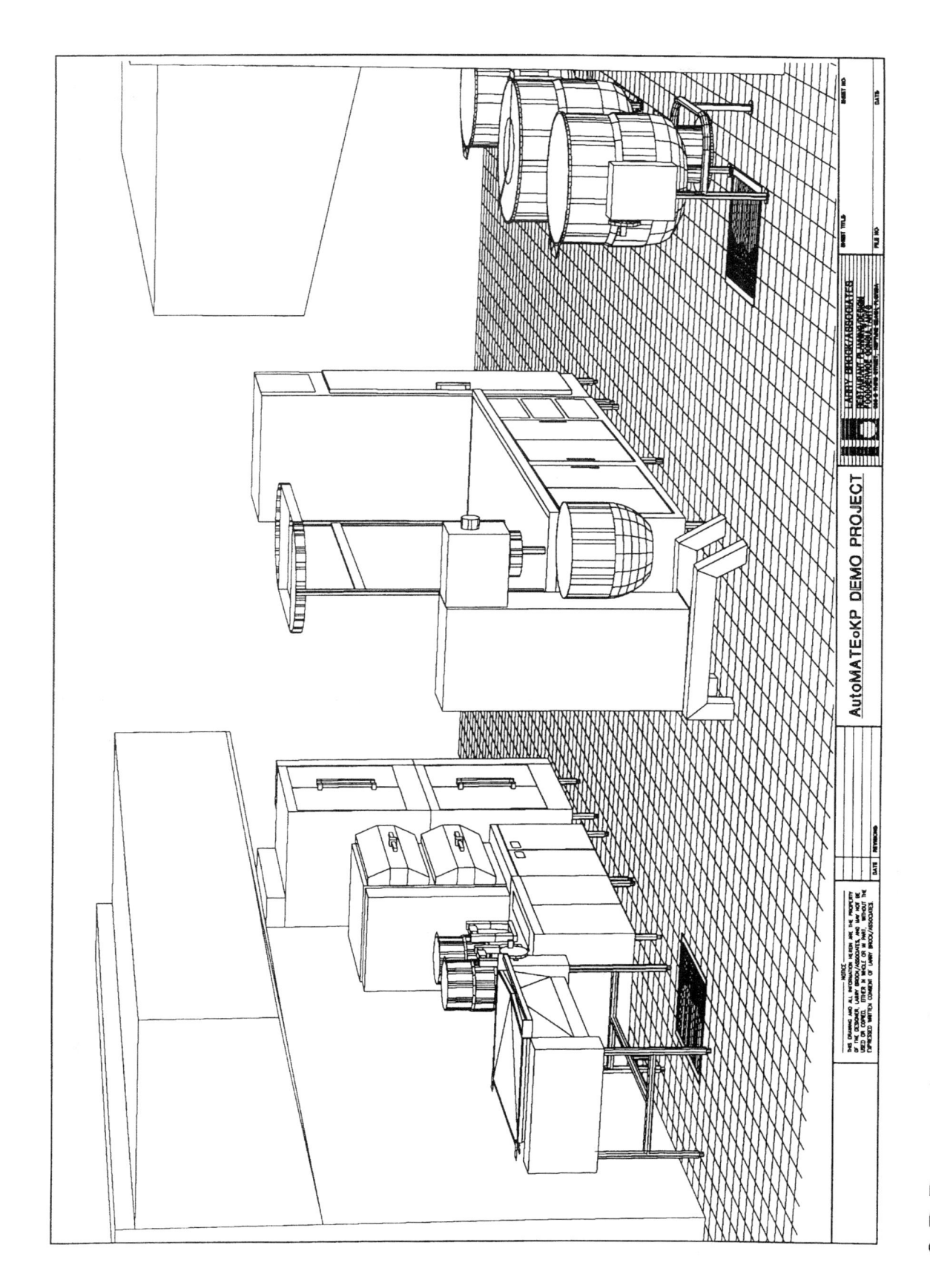

3-D Perspective of Main Cooking Area

3-D Perspective of Bake Shop

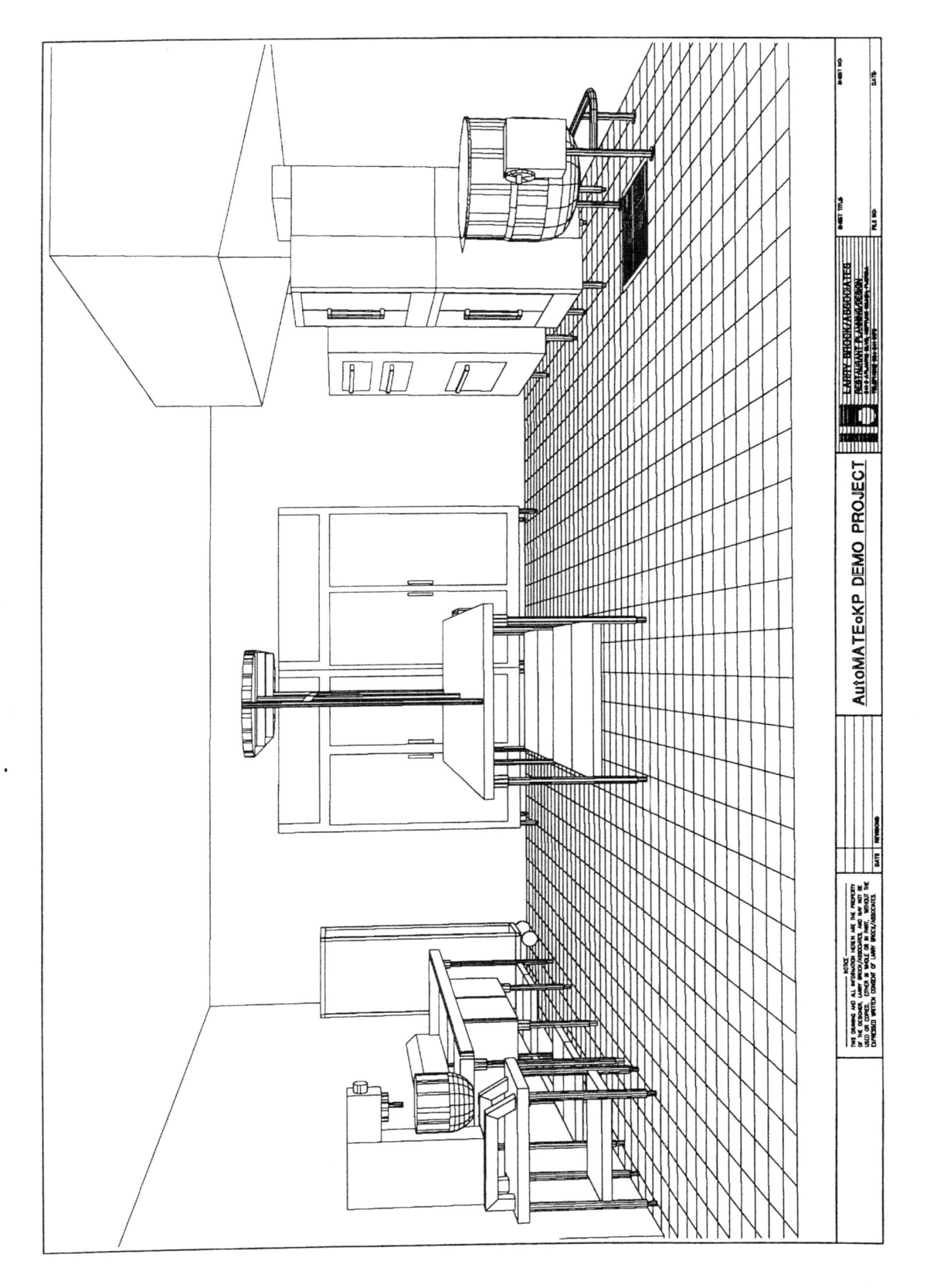

8

Sample Site and Installation Procedures

Correctional Facilities

Equipment selection

There are special problems in the correctional foodservice department that can only be solved with unique equipment. Security is the key problem requiring your consideration. Second, most county jails feed inmates in decentralized (48- to 64-person) day rooms, rather than in the secure-type large cafeteria used by state long term institutions. Third, labor hours are plentiful and at close to zero cost to foodservice. However, control of labor is often a problem. Finally, ask your manufacturers to help write specs for you to protect you from substitution.

Production equipment

Care should be taken when specifying production equipment. Only the most rugged and simple to clean mixers, for example, should be considered. Just because a prison package is offered does not mean a product will work. No loose parts that can be made into weapons should be installed. Electrical areas must be protected; some inmates will try to get a shock, so that they can start a lawsuit. Equipment should be very easy to clean. Inmates try to use a hose to clean everything when supervision is absent. Plan on *extreme abuse* of your equipment.

All complex controls should be avoided. *Keep it simple* is the rule. This means simple, rugged steam kettles and ranges and walk-in refrigerators with windowed doors.

Meal distribution

Use tray distribution systems in county jails and high security state or federal correctional institutions. These are the most unique elements of their equipment packages. They are based on the meal tray chosen by the administration. There are about 10 basic types of trays, but they fall into only three basic areas:

- insulated trays
- heated trays
- heated and refrigerated trays

Of course, the type of plastic tray will determine the type of delivery cart. Tray assembly requires a parallel layout of conveyor, steam tables, and cold units. Simple, easy to clean roller conveyors are always preferred to complex power conveyors. Power outlets should be part of the conveyor.

Don't forget drying racks for the plastic trays. Be careful about selection of the dishwasher. Make sure it is designed with a drying section. Plastic trays use special belts in flight-type dish machines. Plastic trays work best in a low temp unit.

Finally, make sure the equipment has all the optional accessories you require. For example, don't buy only the basic vent hood and miss the fire suppression system that requires specifications and is listed as an option.

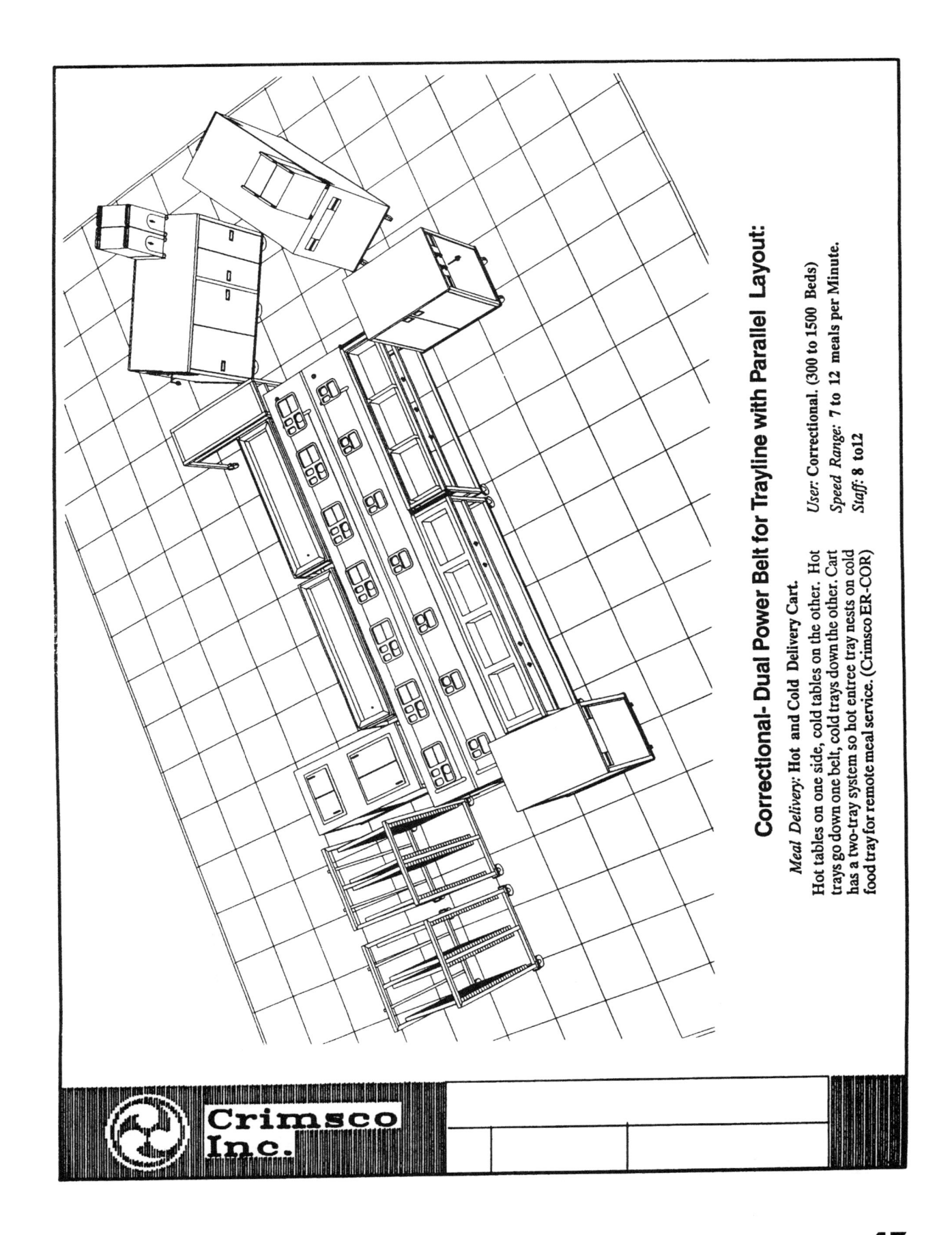

Correctional- Dual Power Belt for Trayline with Parallel Layout:

Meal Delivery: Hot and Cold Delivery Cart.

Hot tables on one side, cold tables on the other. Hot trays go down one belt, cold trays down the other. Cart has a two-tray system so hot entree tray nests on cold food tray for remote meal service. (Crimsco ER-COR)

User: Correctional. (300 to 1500 Beds)
Speed Range: 7 to 12 meals per Minute.
Staff: 8 to 12

Crimsco Inc.

47

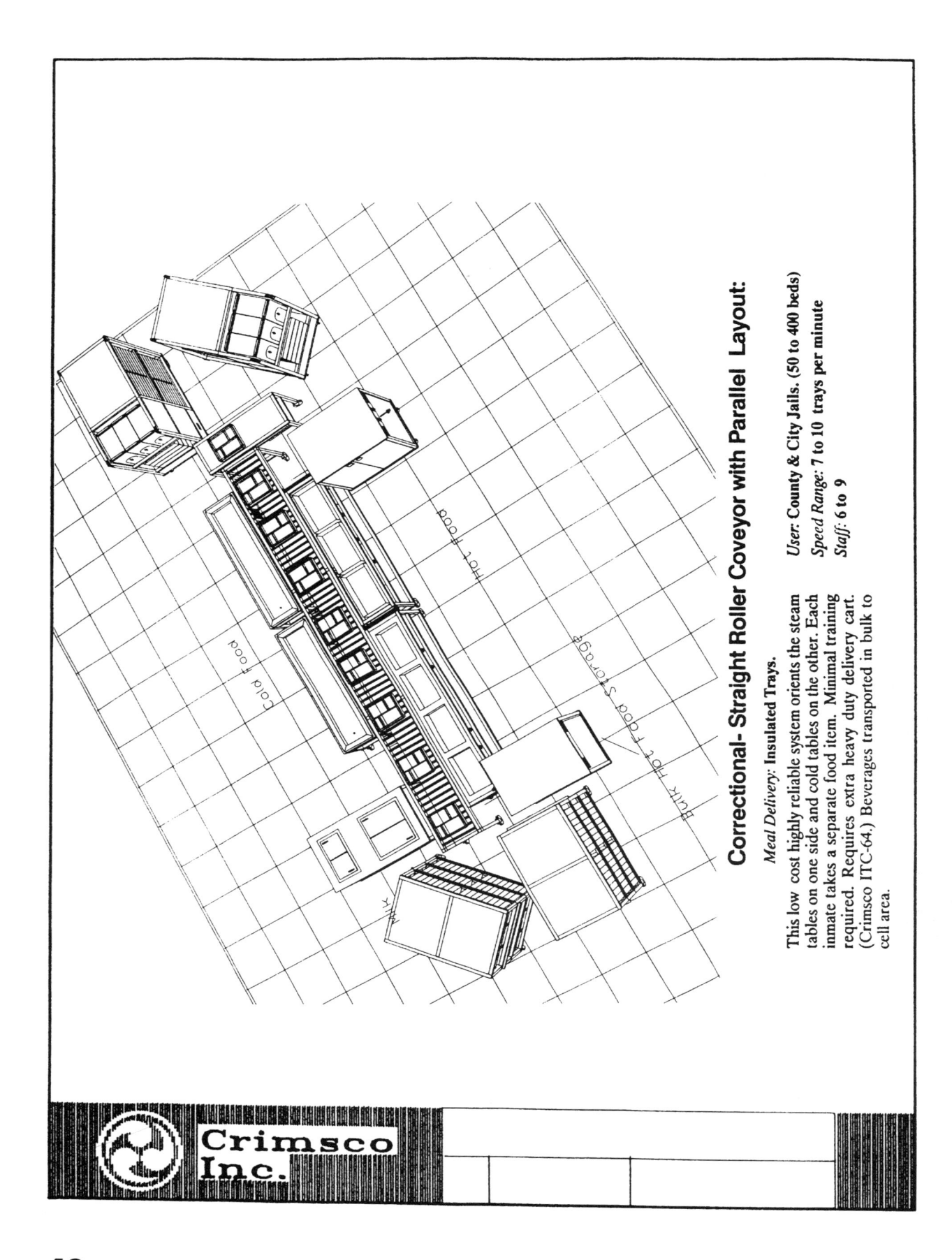

Correctional- Straight Roller Coveyor with Parallel Layout:

Meal Delivery: Insulated Trays.

This low cost highly reliable system orients the steam tables on one side and cold tables on the other. Each inmate takes a separate food item. Minimal training required. Requires extra heavy duty delivery cart. (Crimsco ITC-64.) Beverages transported in bulk to cell area.

User: County & City Jails. (50 to 400 beds)
Speed Range: 7 to 10 trays per minute
Staff: 6 to 9

Crimsco Inc.

Healthcare

EQUIPMENT SELECTION

This market segment has special needs and is divided into acute care and nursing home business. Both require decentralized meal service, and acute care requires cafeteria service as well. The trend is clear in this market: any equipment that allows reduction of labor is of interest. On the other hand, new regulations called "HACCP" concerning food pathogens are becoming significantly important.

PRODUCTION AND DISTRIBUTION EQUIPMENT

The cook/chill production system is being offered as a major labor saving innovation. Cost of this system per patient bed ranges from $600.00 to $1500.00. These systems really require the services of a very experienced consultant. In order to quickly chill hot food for storage, both blast chillers and bag chillers with pumping stations are used. Conventional kitchen production equipment isn't unusual. Healthcare foodservice departments use four types of patient meal distribution: insulated trays and heated bases with insulated domes (passive systems); and hot and cold carts or cook/chill retherm (active systems which are "HACCP" compliant). The new regulations will require hot food to be held at 140°F or higher and cold food to be held at less than 45°F. Dishwashing systems should be designed with special belts when insulated trays or insulated domes are used.

TRAY ASSEMBLY EQUIPMENT

Both acute care hospitals and nursing homes assemble trays for patients. Powered straight or circular tray conveyors are used. Both narrow and wide steam and cold tables are required. Pellet heaters and dome racks are used on some systems. Air curtain refrigerators are a popular method of holding preplated cold items. However, in many nursing homes, a system using hot and cold carts with advance pre-loading of cold trays eliminates the conveyor, saves space, and reduces labor.

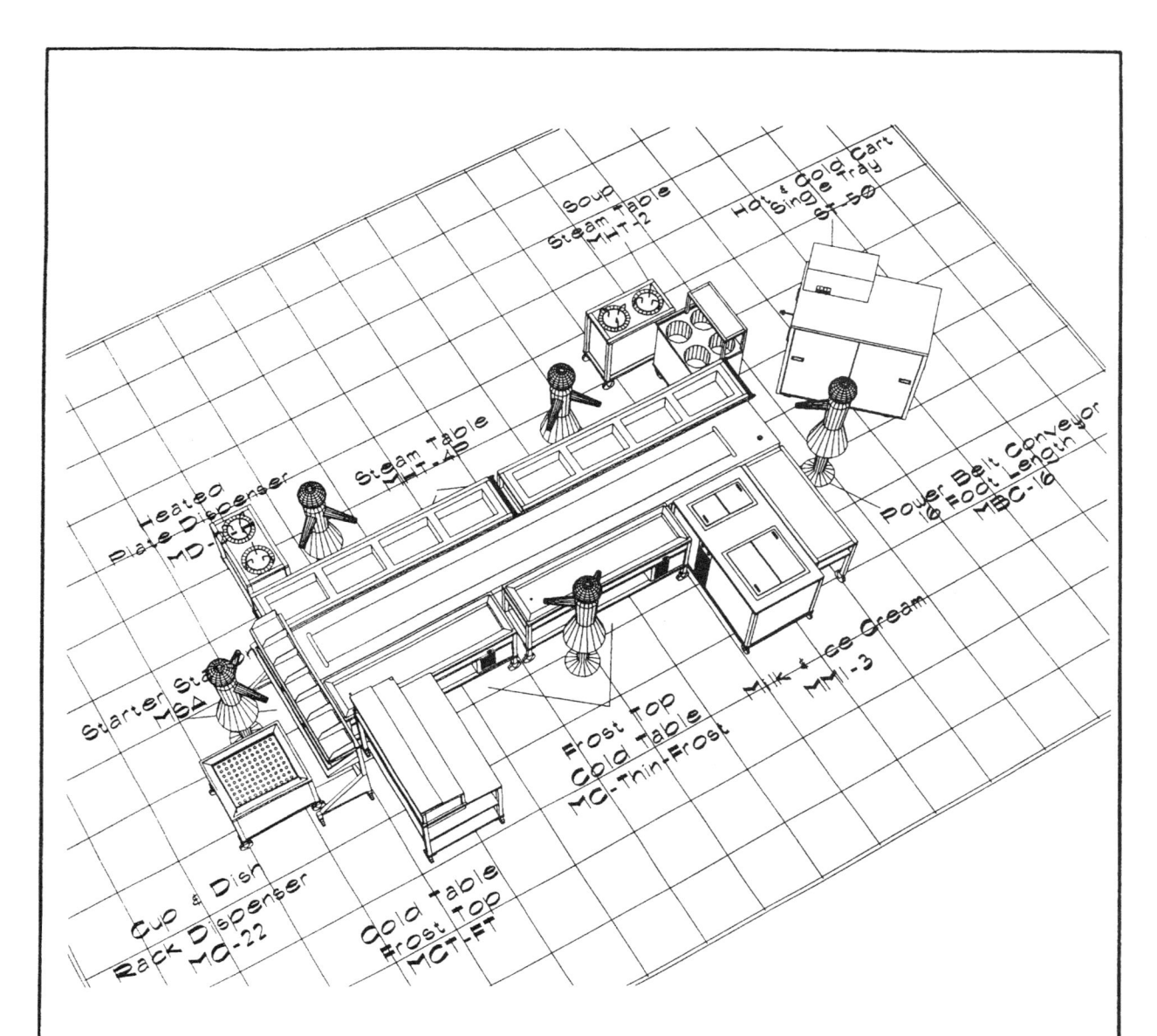

Mid-Sized Hospitals—Straight Powered Belt Conveyor With Parallel Equipment:

Meal Delivery: **Insulated Trays, Pellets, Hot & Cold Carts.**

This is the space saving variant of the straight belt conveyor. It fits into about 15% less space than a comparable circular conveyor. It will cost about one-half the price of a comparable circular conveyor. It may be used very effectively where there are fluctuations in census requiring reduction of trayline positions. Lateral movement of staff means that the belt need not stop as frequently.

Users: **Medium Sized Hospitals and Nursing Homes. (100 to 350 Beds)**
Speed Range: **3.5 to 4.5 trays per minute**
Staff: **6 to 7**

Crimsco Inc.

Circular Conveyor With Parallel Mobile Support Equipment:

Meal Delivery: Pellet System.

This is a very expensive solution to the trayline layout problem. By using mobile parallel support equipment, a flexible approach is possible. The flexibility of the mobile support equipment means that as your census and menu changes, you can re-lay your trayline to meet new conditions. The parallel layout of the hot and cold equipment means staffing of positions also vary with the census, up or down. This layout is the second most space efficient. Built in hot and cold stations **not** recommended.

Users: **Large Hospitals. (450 to 1,500 Beds)**
Speed Range: **3 to 5 trays per minute**
Staff: **8 to 9**

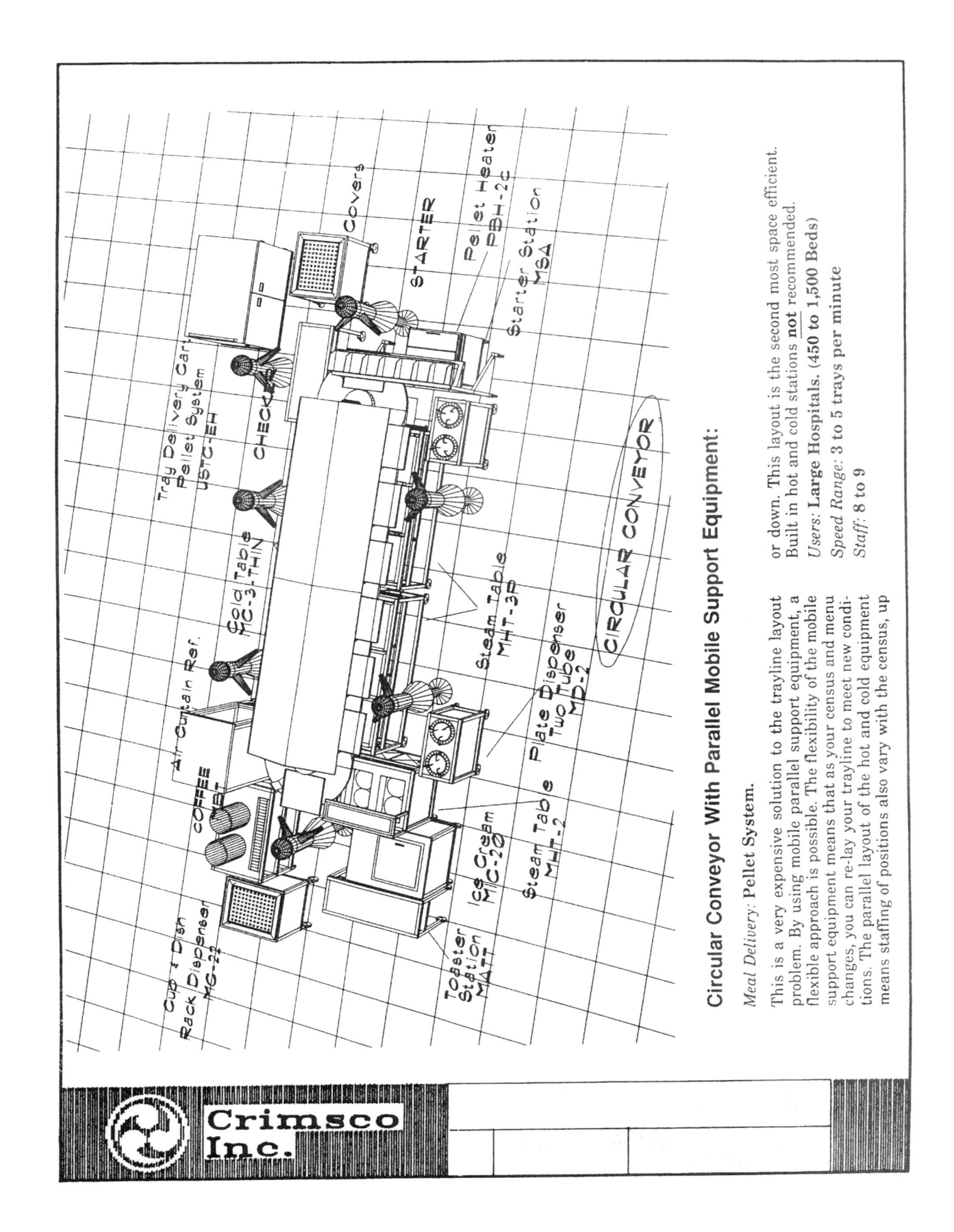

Nursing Home-Tray Assembly Without a Conveyor:

Meal Delivery: **Hot and Cold Carts.**

Uses advance pre-loading of cold trays into cold section of cart. Later, hot meals are plated and loaded into heated section of cart just prior to dispatch.(Crimsco ER-CC Cart.) Plate heaters necessary, includes steam table, cold table, tray and dish dispensers.

User: **Nursing Homes.** (60 to 160 beds)
Speed: **2.5 to 3.5** meals per minute
Staff: **2 to 3**

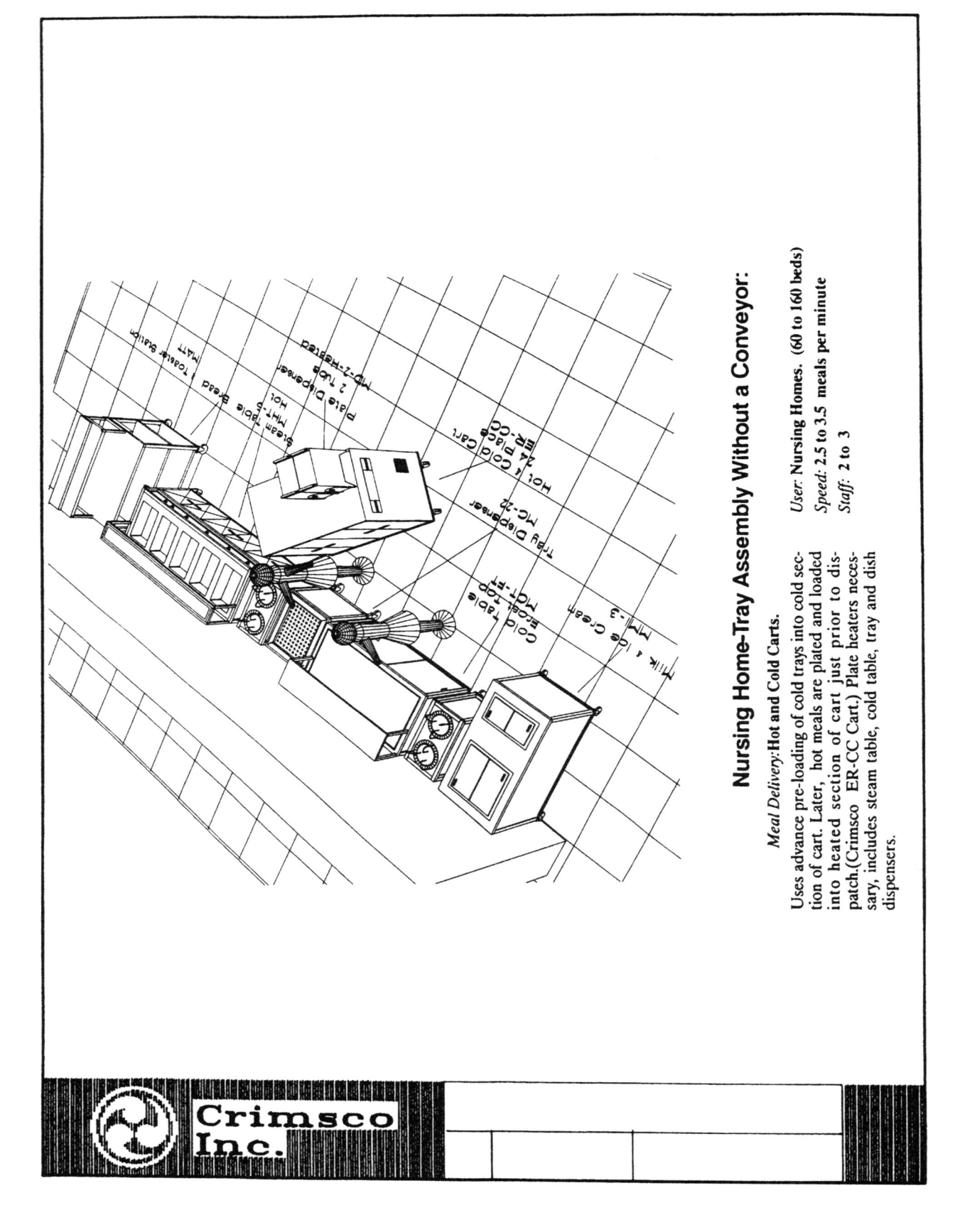

Crimsco Inc.

(1) Zoning
    Current zoning of site
    Use permits needed
    Height restrictions
    Front line set back
    Side yard requirements
    Back yard requirements
    Restrictions on signs
    Parking requirements
    Other restrictions
(2) Area Characteristics
    Type of neighborhood
    Type of businesses
    Growth pattern
    Proposed construction
    Other available sites
    Zoning of adjacent sites
(3) Competition
    Number of food facilities in drawing area of site
    Number of seats
    Type of menu offered
    Method of service
    Check averages
    Number of cocktail lounges
    Quality of drinks
    Bar service available at tables
    Annual sales
(4) Physical characteristics
    Type of top soil
    Type of subsoil
    Depth of water table
    Presence of rocks
    Load-bearing capacity
    Direction of slopes
    Surface drainage
    Percolation test results
    Natural landscaping
    Other features
(5) Size and Shape (Including sketch)
    Length
    Width
    Total square feet
    Square footage needed for building
    Square footage needed for parking
    Space for other requirements
(6) Costs
    Cost per front foot
    Cost per square foot
    Total cost of site
    Cost of comparable sites nearby
    Costs for land improvements
    Real estate taxes
    Other taxes
(7) Utilities
    Location, cost, and size or capacity of:
        Storm sewer
        Sanitary sewer
        Gas lines
        Water lines
        Electricity
        Steam
(8) Streets
    Basic patterns
    Width or lanes
    Paved
    Curbs and gutters
    Sidewalks
    Lighting
    Public transportation
    Grades
    Hazards
(9) Positional Characteristics
    Distance and driving time to: Distance   Driving Time
        Central business district
        Industrial centers
        Shopping centers
        Residential areas
        Recreational areas
        Sporting events
        Educational facilities
        Special attractions
        Other activity generators
(10) Traffic Information
    Distance to nearest intersection
    Traffic characteristics
    Traffic counts: Day   Time   Count
        Site street
        Adjacent streets
    Anticipated changes
(11) Visibility
    Distances of sight from:
        Left
        Right
        Across
    Obstructions
    Location of signs
(12) Availability of local labor
(13) Services
    Quality of police protection
    Quality of fire protection
    Location of hydrant
    Availability of trash pick up
    Availability of garbage pick up
    Other services required
(14) General Recommendations
    Suitability
    Desirability
    Other recommendations

Site analysis worksheet.

Scheduling Equipment Installation

After a project has been bid and/or negotiations for the foodservice equipment have been completed, the critical path to successful installation and production generally follows these guidelines.

The architect leads the team, and the foodservice designer or consultant prepares final plans, locating all plumbing, electric, and ventilation requirements. The schedule included on the drawings will enable the architect's electrical; plumbing; and heating, ventilating, and air conditioning engineers to prepare necessary drawings and specifications. The architectural staff, in the meantime, will have been preparing all of the structural detail plans, including excavation, landscaping, plumbing, and electric rough-ins, building sectional details, elevations, and the many drawings required to make the job complete.

Complete shop drawings must be submitted for all fabricated equipment. The supplier now becomes responsible for any subsequent drawings and submittals. Revised drawings may be required to conform to the specification and/or architectural details. Usually, four or five weeks will be allowed for the kitchen equipment dealer to submit the necessary documents.

Once all submittals have received final approval, fabricated equipment will be put into production. Some fabricated items may take up to 12–14 weeks to be delivered. Some of the fabricated items may be too large to fit through standard doors, and must be brought into the area before walls are completed. This point must always be verified and never overlooked.

When the general contractor completes work in the food service area, including mechanical and electric rough-ins, the equipment contractor will deliver the foodservice equipment, uncrate it, and set it in place. Large pieces may be set in place and field-welded. Internal electric and plumbing connections are usually the responsibility of the kitchen equipment contractor. The general contractor's trades-people make the final connections. A final checklist is completed, reviewing all equipment in regard to compliance with specifications and bid documents. Any deviations are noted and must be corrected. It is important to note code violations and have them corrected. A point that is often overlooked—but should be included in the specifications—is that the equipment be demonstrated. All kitchen employees should be trained in the safety, use, and cleaning of the equipment; thus maximizing the value of the equipment. An owner's manual, including a parts list, warranties, and a list of service agencies with telephone numbers is an additional asset for the owner's future reference and adds to the closing of a successful project.

Banquet Equipment Guide

Selecting Equipment for a Banquet Kitchen

Meals	Convection Oven	Kettle	Convection Steamer	Tilting Fry Pan
50	½	(1) 20 gal.	1 double	(1) 30 gal.
100	½	(1) 20 gal.	1 double	(1) 30 gal.
150	1	(1) 20 gal.	1 double	(1) 30 gal.
200	1	(1) 20 gal.	1 double	(1) 30 gal.
250	1	(1) 30 gal.	2 double	(1) 30–35 gal.
300	1	(1) 30 gal.	2 double	(1) 30–35 gal.
350	1	(1) 40 gal.	2 double	(1) 40 gal.
400	2	(1) 40 gal.	2 double	(1) 40 gal.
450	2	(1) 60 gal.	2 double	(1) 40 gal.
500	2	(1) 60 gal.	2 double	(1) 40 gal.
600	2	(1) 60 gal.	2 double	(1) 40 & (1) 20 gal.
750	3	(2) 40 gal.	2 double	(1) 40 & (1) 20 gal.

Meals required	50–250	250–400	450–600	750
Coffee	Twin 3	Twin 6	Twin 10	Twin 10
Ice	200 lb.	400 lb.	600 lb.	1000 lb.
Servers	2	3	6	8

Average of 20 cups per gallon, 1½ cup per meal.

If there are meeting rooms, add 3 lb. ice per seat.

Heated carts are relatively simple to size since most manufacturers advertise them by dish capacity. Keep in mind is that it is better to provide as many different size carts as possible, since the number of people at a function will vary up to the banquet room capacity.

10
Sanitizing Guide

Bowl Size	Water Depth	Bleach Solution
10" × 14"	10"	.79 oz.
14" × 16"	12"	1.50 oz.
16" × 20"	12"	2.00 oz.
20" × 20"	12"	2.60 oz.
24" × 24"	12"	3.20 oz.
20" × 28"	12"	3.60 oz.

11

Sample Food Equipment Layout Plans

Food Equipment Digest

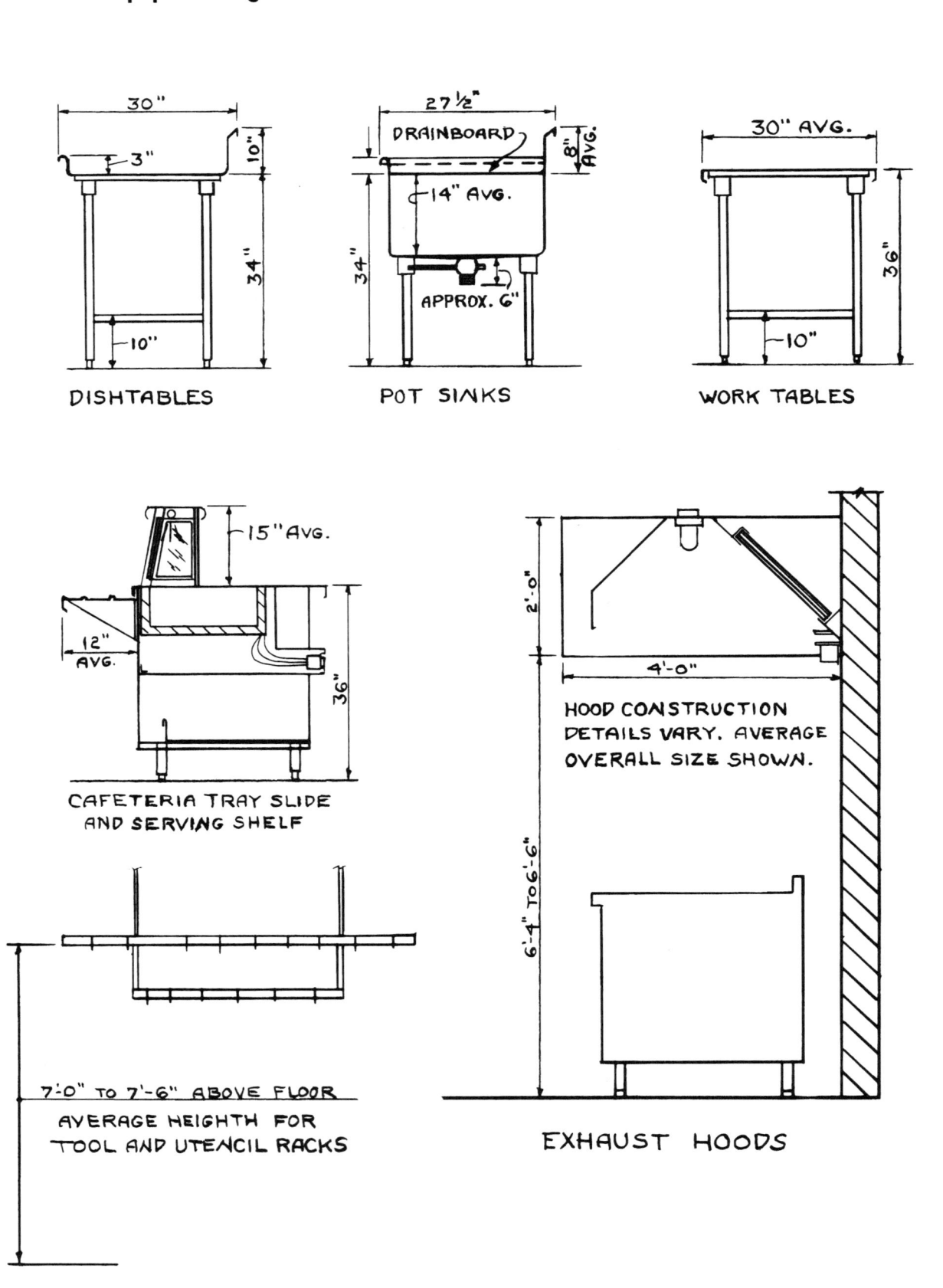

DISHTABLES
- 30"
- 3"
- 10"
- 34"
- 10"

POT SINKS
- 27½"
- DRAINBOARD
- 8" AVG.
- 14" AVG.
- 34"
- APPROX. 6"

WORK TABLES
- 30" AVG.
- 36"
- 10"

CAFETERIA TRAY SLIDE AND SERVING SHELF
- 15" AVG.
- 12" AVG.
- 36"

7'-0" TO 7'-6" ABOVE FLOOR
AVERAGE HEIGHTH FOR TOOL AND UTENCIL RACKS

EXHAUST HOODS
- 2'-0"
- 4'-0"
- 6'-4" TO 6'-6"

HOOD CONSTRUCTION DETAILS VARY. AVERAGE OVERALL SIZE SHOWN.

Sample Food Equipment Layout Plans **61**

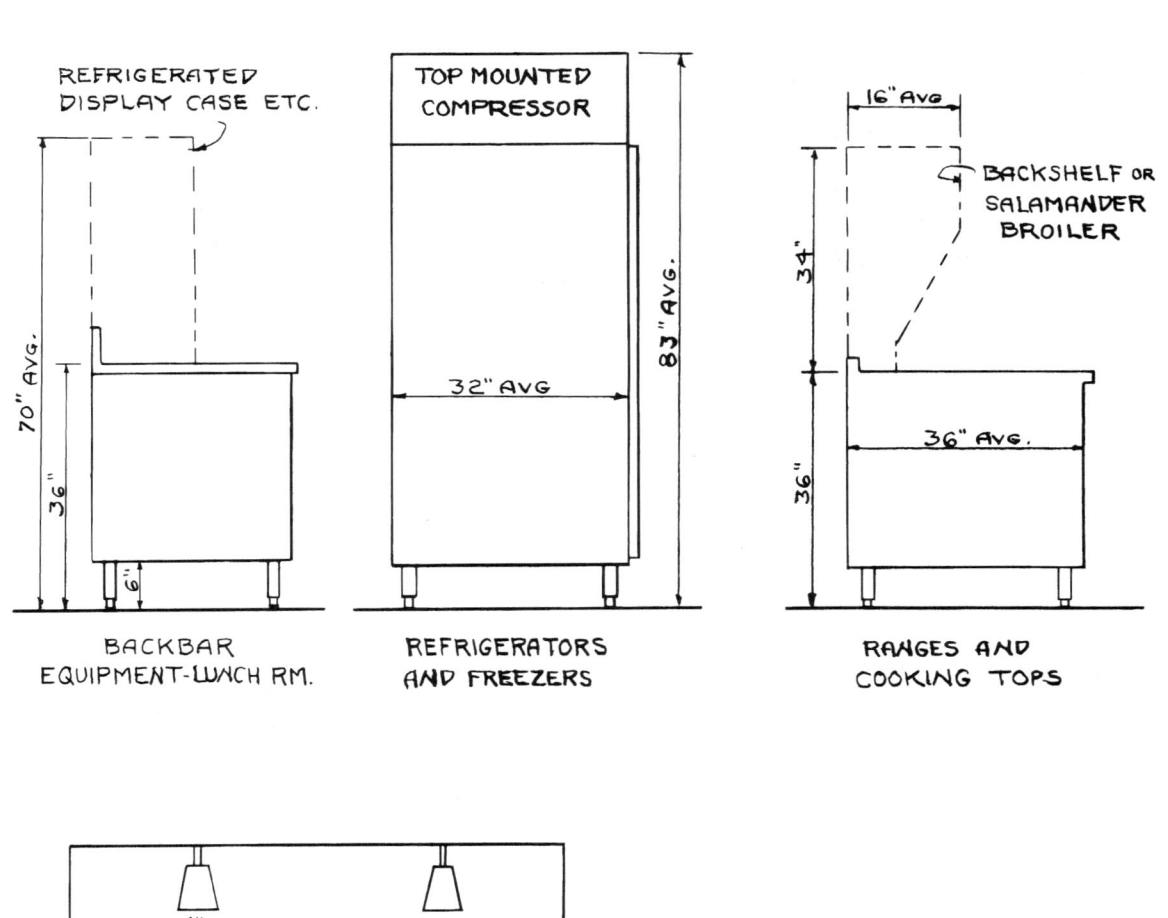

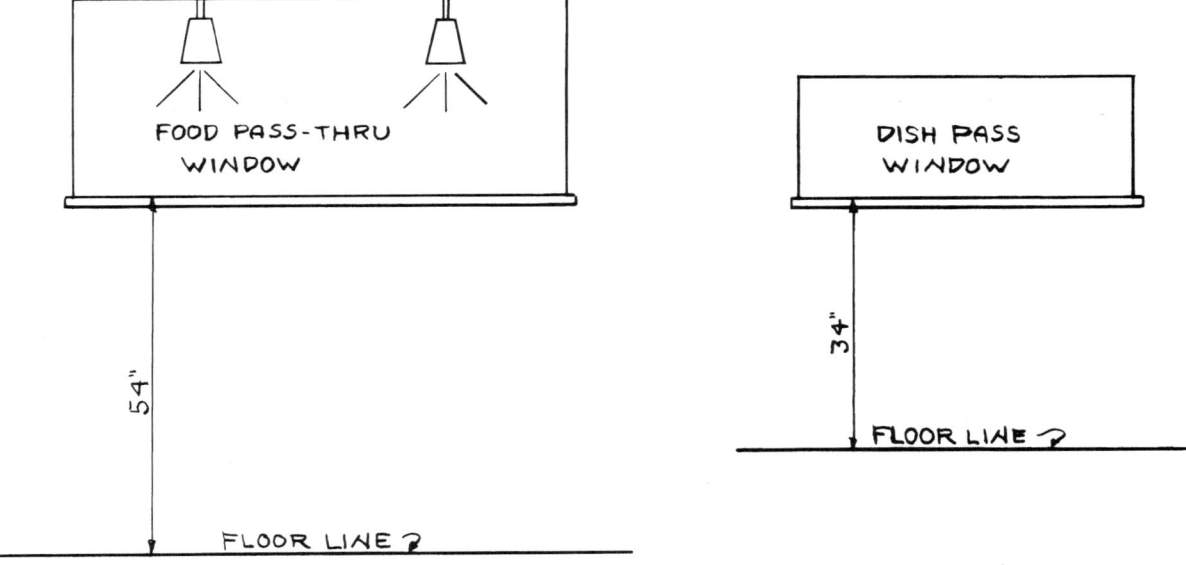

REFRIGERATED DISPLAY CASE ETC.

70" AVG.
36"
6"

BACKBAR EQUIPMENT-LUNCH RM.

TOP MOUNTED COMPRESSOR

83" AVG.
32" AVG

REFRIGERATORS AND FREEZERS

16" AVG
BACKSHELF OR SALAMANDER BROILER

34"
36" AVG.
36"

RANGES AND COOKING TOPS

FOOD PASS-THRU WINDOW

54"

FLOOR LINE ?

DISH PASS WINDOW

34"

FLOOR LINE ?

LUNCH COUNTER

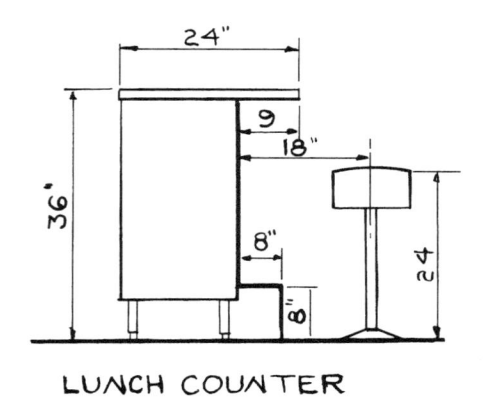

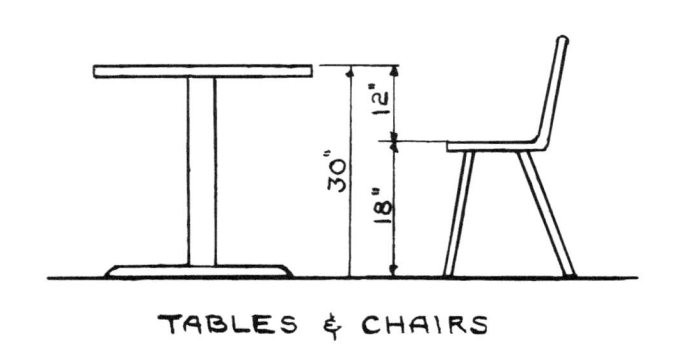

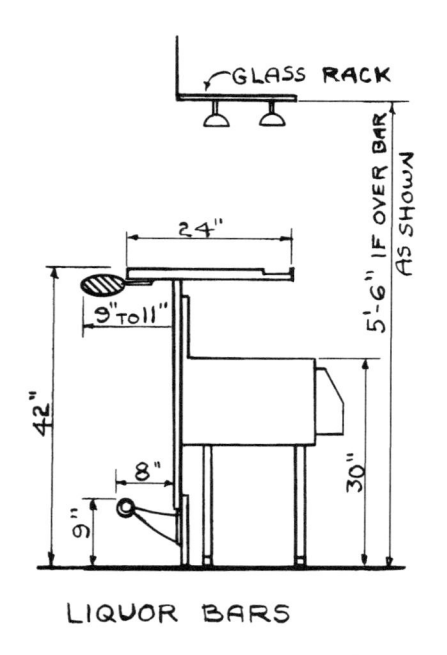

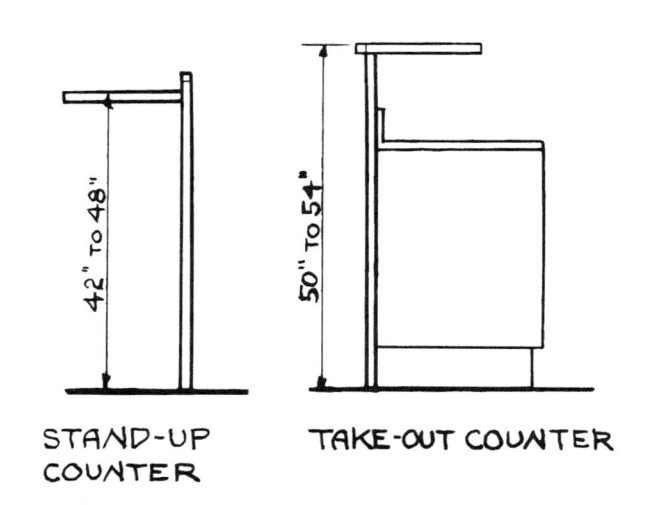

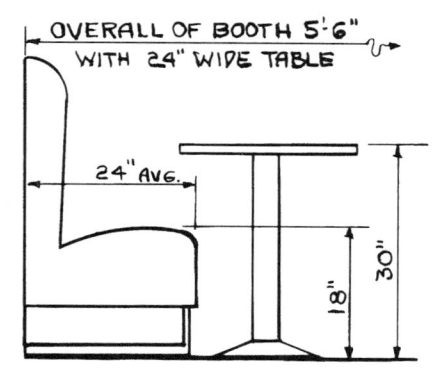

- 24" counter width
- 36" counter height
- 18" / 9" dimensions
- 8" kick
- 24" stool height
- 8" toe space

TABLES & CHAIRS

- 30" table height
- 18" seat height
- 12" from seat to table

LIQUOR BARS

- GLASS RACK
- 5'-6" IF OVER BAR AS SHOWN
- 24" bar top
- 9" to 11"
- 42" bar height
- 30" back bar
- 8" / 9" toe

STAND-UP COUNTER

- 42" to 48"

TAKE-OUT COUNTER

- 50" to 54"

TYPICAL BOOTH DIMENSIONS

- OVERALL OF BOOTH 5'-6" WITH 24" WIDE TABLE
- 24" AVE.
- 30" table height
- 18" seat height

AVERAGE SPACE ALLOCATION IN DINING ROOMS IS FROM 10 TO 15 SQ. FT. PER PERSON.
10☐' PER PERSON WOULD BE TIGHT BANQUET SEATING.
12☐' PER PERSON IS AVERAGE.
15☐' PER PERSON TENDS TO LUXURIOUS.

Sample Food Equipment Layout Plans

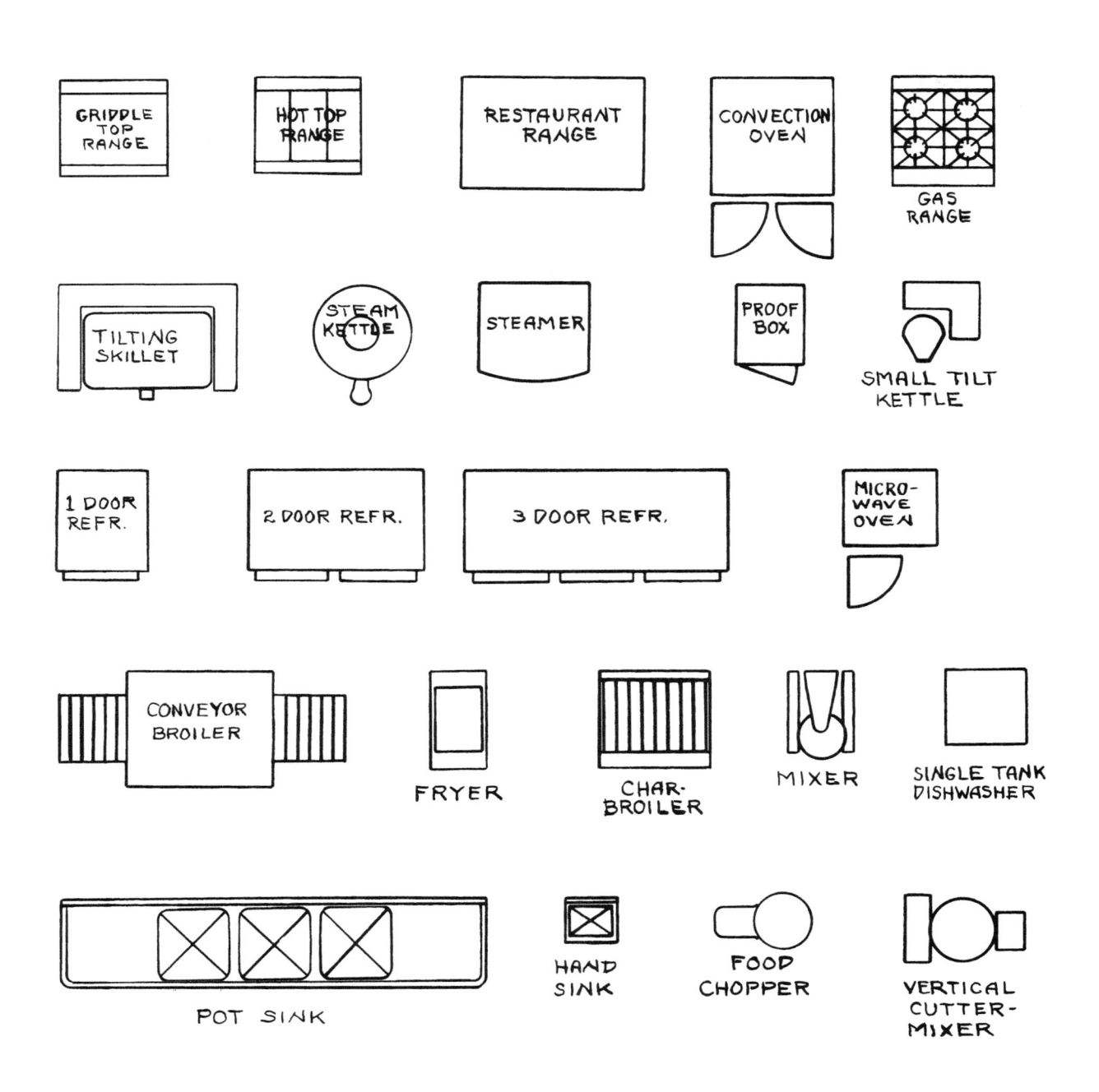

Food equipment templates.

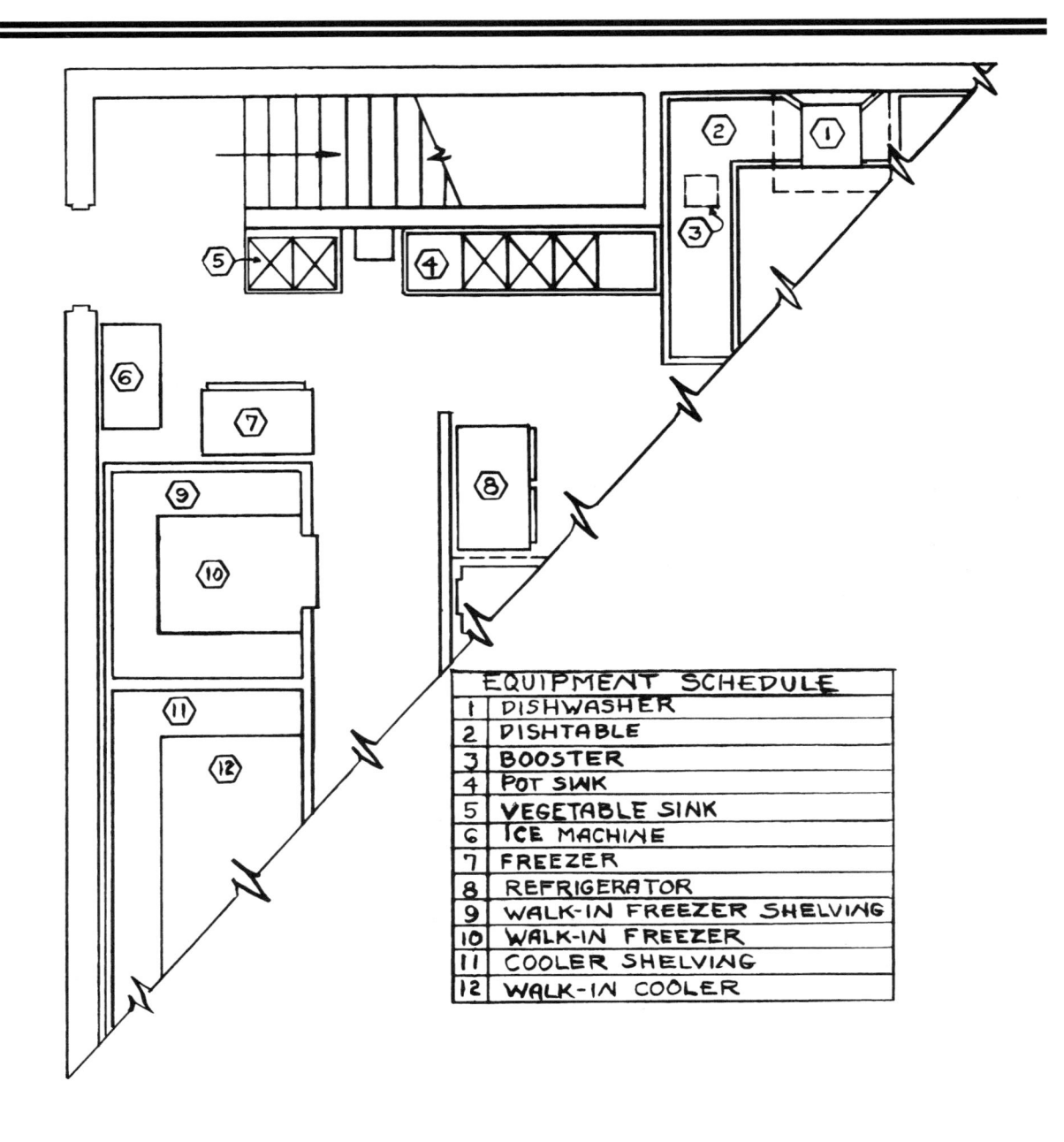

EQUIPMENT SCHEDULE	
1	DISHWASHER
2	DISHTABLE
3	BOOSTER
4	POT SINK
5	VEGETABLE SINK
6	ICE MACHINE
7	FREEZER
8	REFRIGERATOR
9	WALK-IN FREEZER SHELVING
10	WALK-IN FREEZER
11	COOLER SHELVING
12	WALK-IN COOLER

Sample plumbing rough-in plan.

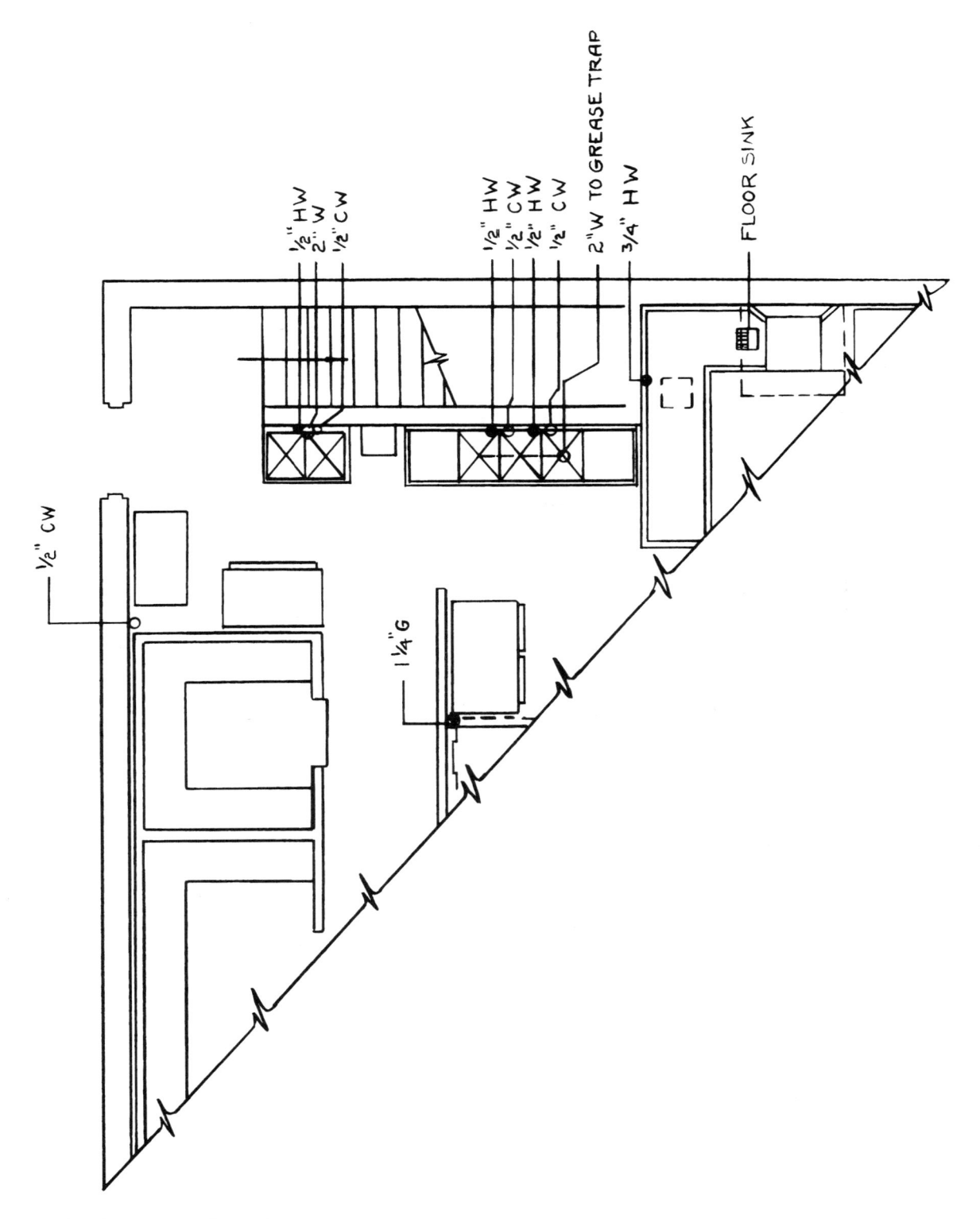

Sample electric rough-in plan.

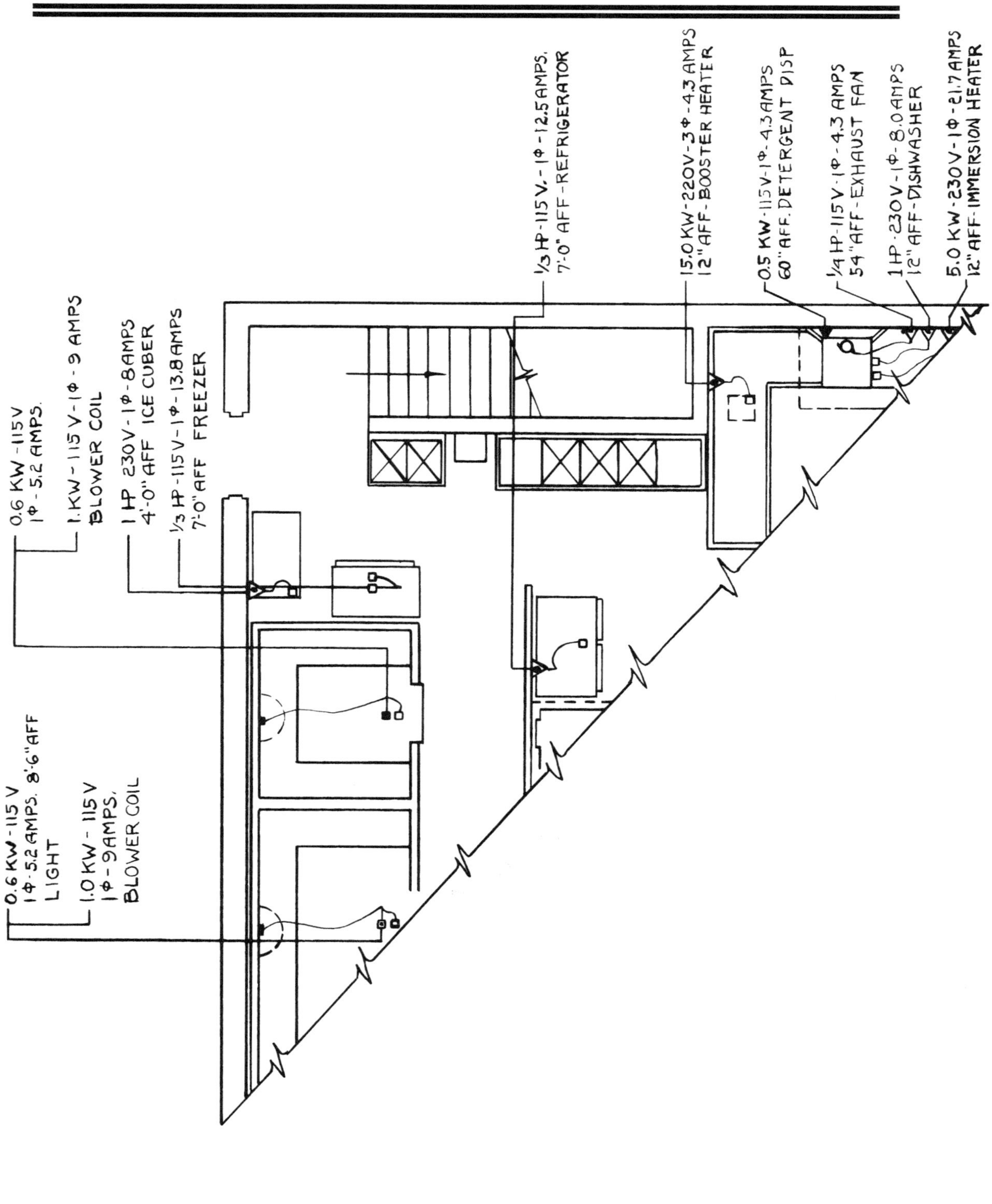
0.6 KW-115 V
1Φ-5.2 AMPS. 8'6"AFF
LIGHT
1.0 KW - 115 V
1Φ - 9AMPS,
BLOWER COIL
0.6 KW -115 V
1Φ - 5.2 AMPS.
1.KW - 115 V - 1Φ - 9 AMPS
BLOWER COIL
1 HP 230V - 1Φ - 8AMPS
4'-0" AFF ICE CUBER
1/3 HP -115V - 1Φ - 13.8 AMPS
7'-0" AFF FREEZER
1/3 HP-115 V.- 1Φ - 12.5 AMPS.
7'-0" AFF - REFRIGERATOR
15.0 KW-220V-3Φ - 4.3 AMPS
12" AFF-BOOSTER HEATER
0.5 KW-115V-1Φ-4.3AMPS
60" AFF. DETERGENT DISP
1/4 HP-115V-1Φ-4.3 AMPS
54"AFF-EXHAUST FAN
1 HP-230V-1Φ-8.0AMPS
12" AFF-DISHWASHER
5.0 KW-230V-1Φ-21.7AMPS
12"AFF-IMMERSION HEATER

Sample Food Equipment Layout Plans

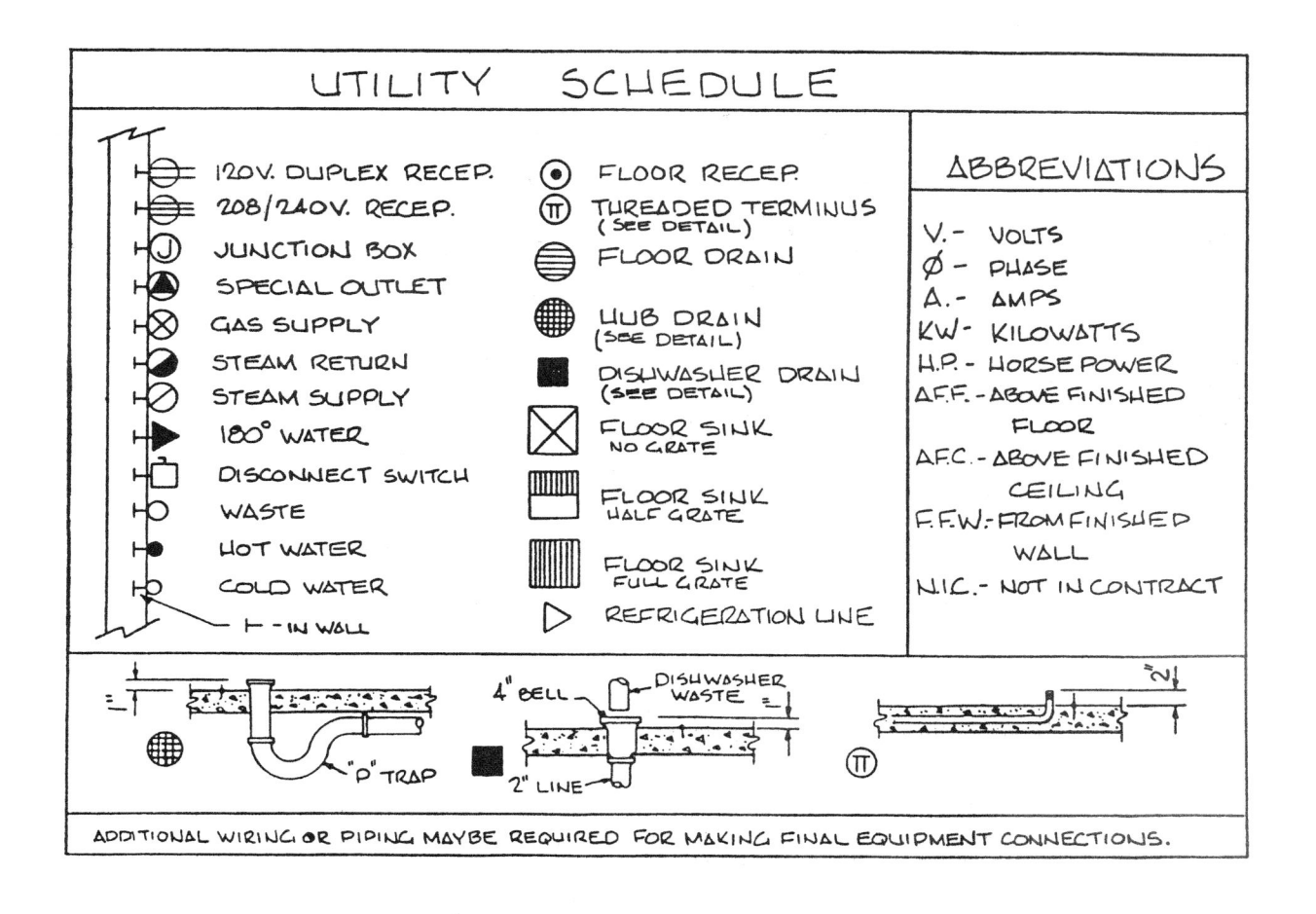

UTILITY SCHEDULE

Symbol	Description	Symbol	Description
⊖	120V. DUPLEX RECEP.	⊙	FLOOR RECEP.
⊜	208/240V. RECEP.	(π)	THREADED TERMINUS (SEE DETAIL)
(J)	JUNCTION BOX	⊜	FLOOR DRAIN
▲	SPECIAL OUTLET	⊕	HUB DRAIN (SEE DETAIL)
⊗	GAS SUPPLY	■	DISHWASHER DRAIN (SEE DETAIL)
◐	STEAM RETURN	⊠	FLOOR SINK NO GRATE
⊘	STEAM SUPPLY		FLOOR SINK HALF GRATE
▶	180° WATER		FLOOR SINK FULL GRATE
□	DISCONNECT SWITCH	▷	REFRIGERATION LINE
○	WASTE		
●	HOT WATER		
○	COLD WATER		
⊢	IN WALL		

ABBREVIATIONS

- V. – VOLTS
- ∅ – PHASE
- A. – AMPS
- KW – KILOWATTS
- H.P. – HORSEPOWER
- A.F.F. – ABOVE FINISHED FLOOR
- A.F.C. – ABOVE FINISHED CEILING
- F.F.W. – FROM FINISHED WALL
- N.I.C. – NOT IN CONTRACT

ADDITIONAL WIRING OR PIPING MAYBE REQUIRED FOR MAKING FINAL EQUIPMENT CONNECTIONS.

68 Food Equipment Digest

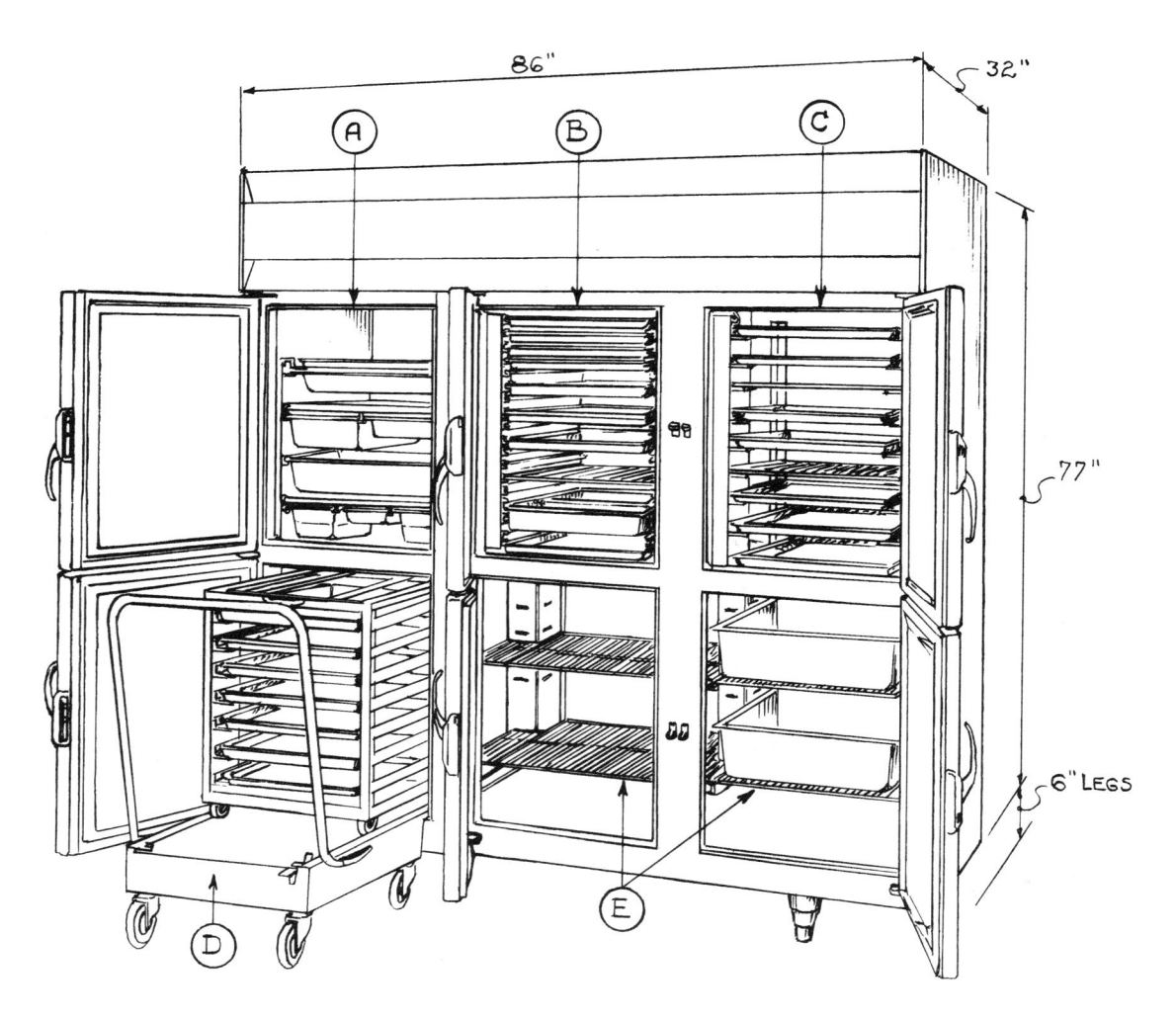

A. PAN GLIDES FOR 12 X 20 AND FRACTIONAL FOOD SERVICE PANS
B. PAN GLIDES FOR 18 X 26 FOOD SERVICE PANS
C. UNIVERSAL PAN GLIDES FITS MOST STANDARD PANS
D. TRANSPORT TRUCK MODULE 18 X 26 PANS
E. STANDARD WIRE SHELVING

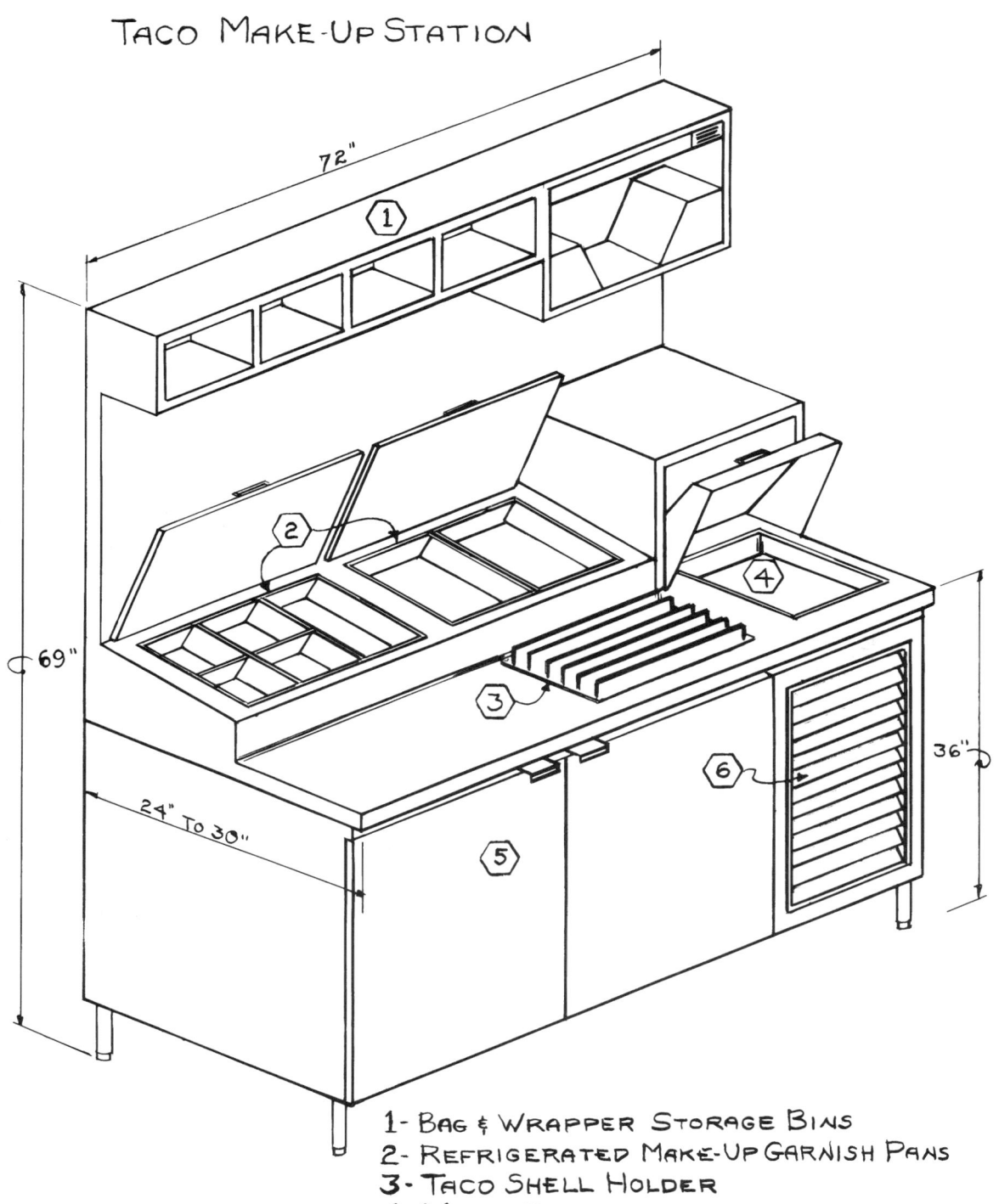

Sample Food Equipment Layout Plans **69**

TACO MAKE-UP STATION

72"
69"
24" TO 30"
36"

1 - BAG & WRAPPER STORAGE BINS
2 - REFRIGERATED MAKE-UP GARNISH PANS
3 - TACO SHELL HOLDER
4 - MEAT PAN
5 - REFRIGERATED BASE
6 - COMPRESSOR HOUSING

LEGEND

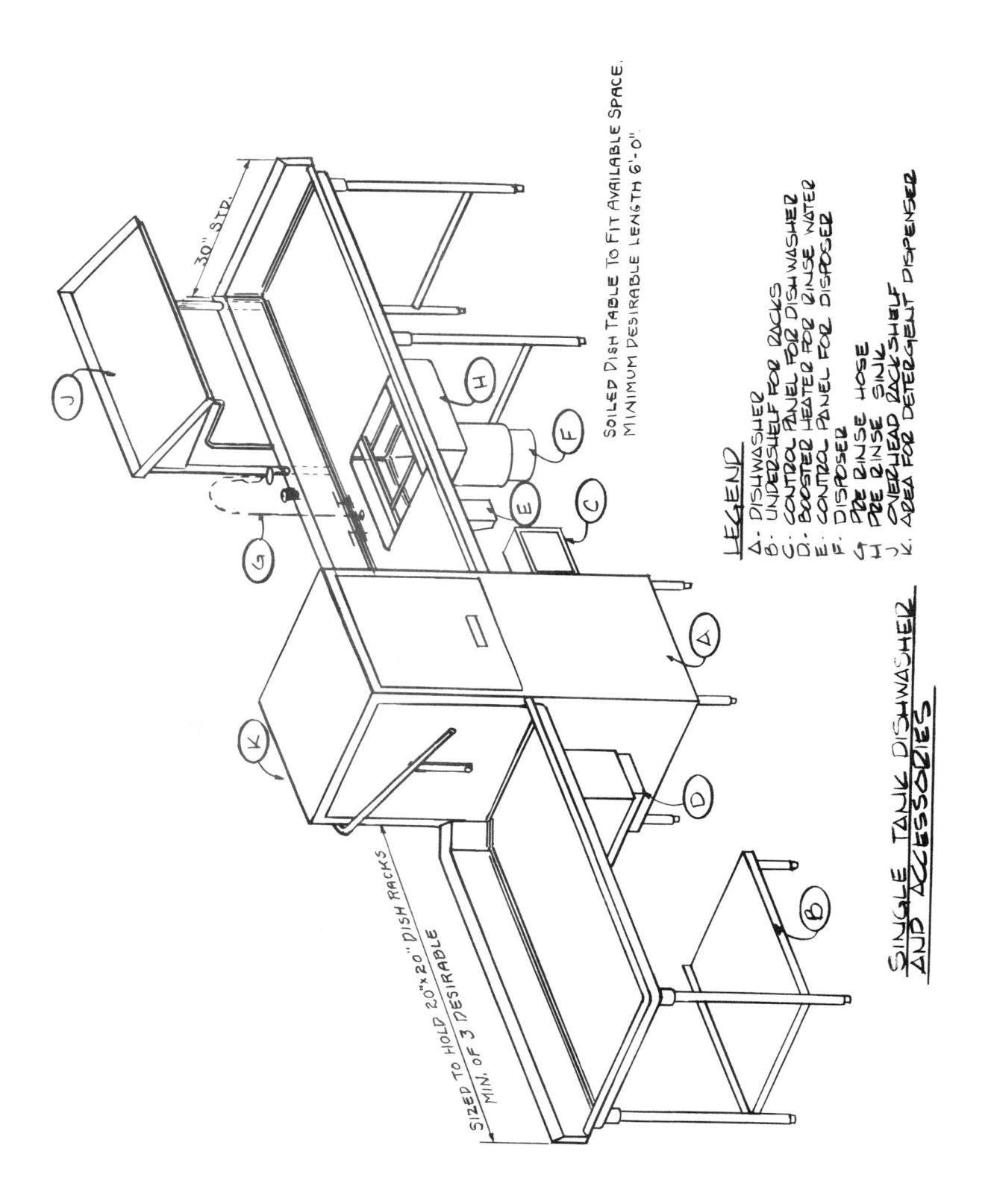

A. DISHWASHER
B. UNDERSHELF FOR RACKS
C. CONTROL PANEL FOR DISHWASHER
D. BOOSTER HEATER FOR RINSE WATER
E. CONTROL PANEL FOR DISPOSER
F. DISPOSER
G. PRE RINSE HOSE
H. PRE RINSE SINK
J. OVERHEAD RACKSHELF
K. AREA FOR DETERGENT DISPENSER

SOILED DISH TABLE TO FIT AVAILABLE SPACE. MINIMUM DESIRABLE LENGTH 6'-0"

30" STD.

SIZED TO HOLD 20"x20" DISH RACKS MIN. OF 3 DESIRABLE

SINGLE TANK DISHWASHER AND ACCESSORIES

70

LEGEND

A. HEAT LAMP
B. DUMP STATION FOR FRYS
C. BAG HOLDER
D. DRINK DISPENSER
E. STORAGE BASE
F. CUP DISPENSER
G. HEATED STORAGE
H. HEATED SANDWICH RACK
J. WRAP STATION
K. STORAGE
L. TOASTER
M. GARNISH OR SANDWICH UNIT
N. HOT PAN ROLLER
O. REFRIGERATED BASE
P. COMPRESSOR HOUSING

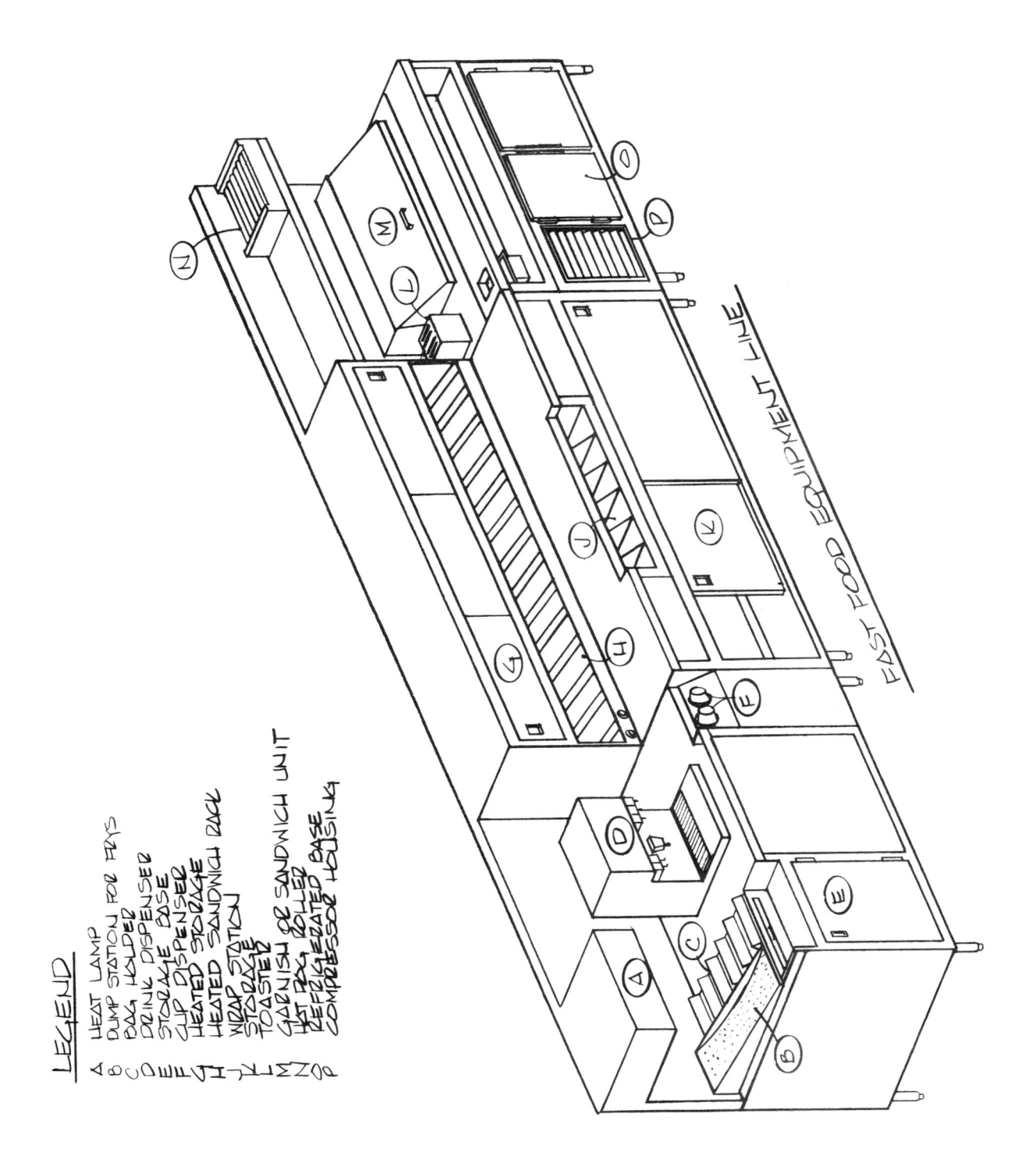

FAST FOOD EQUIPMENT LINE

FRYERS - GRILL AND SANDWICH AREA

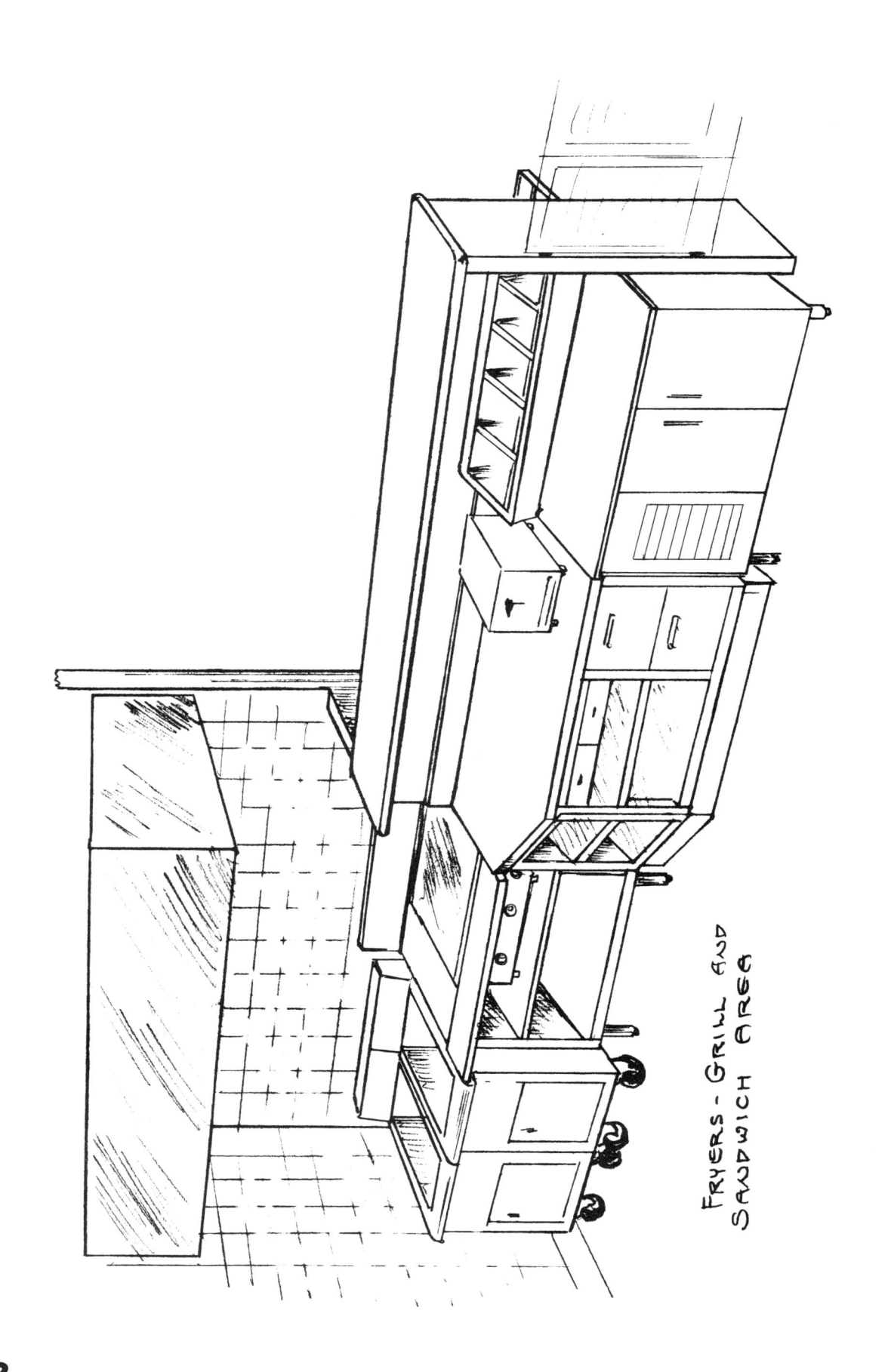

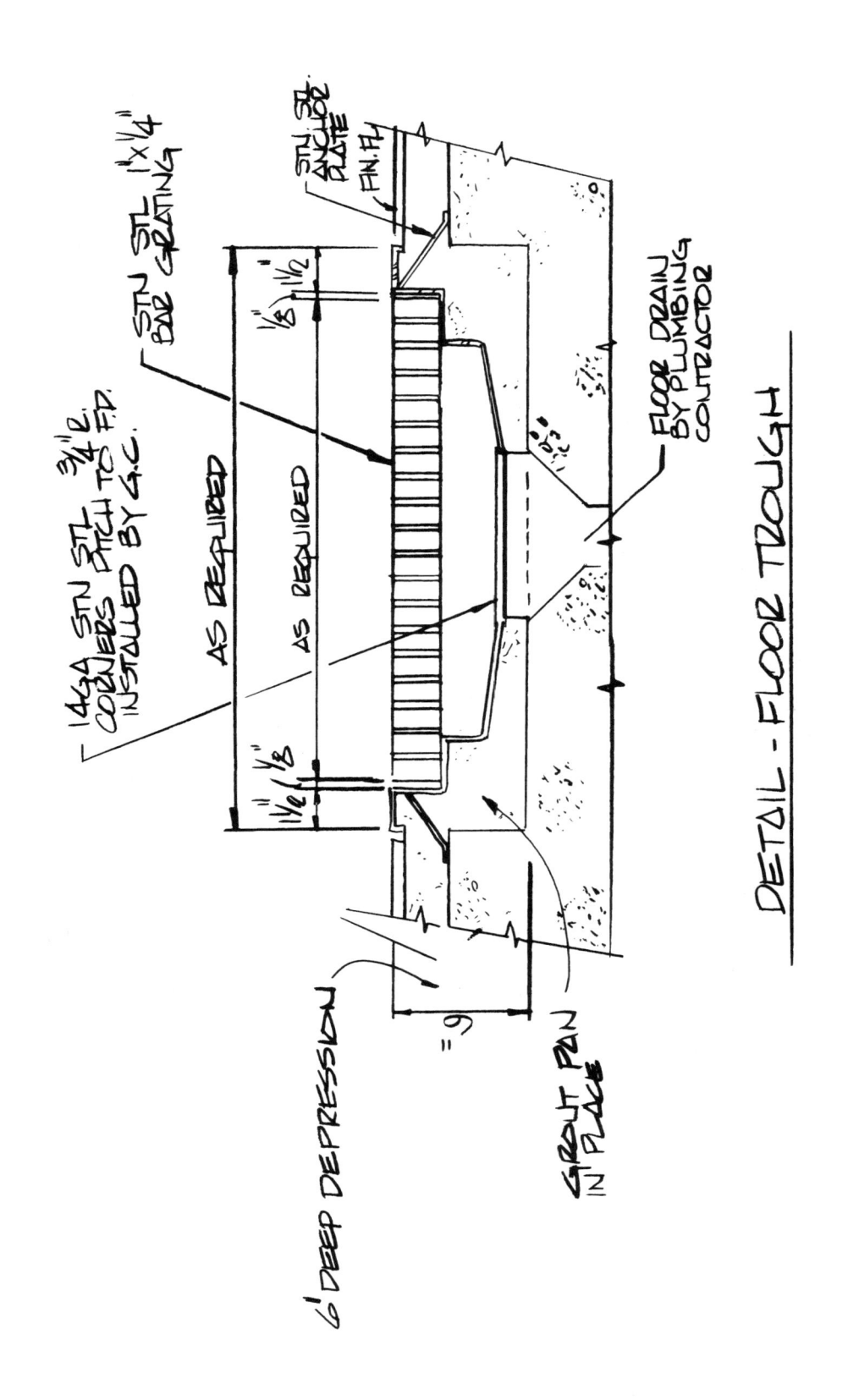

14GA STN. STL. 3/4" R. CORNERS PITCH TO F.D. INSTALLED BY G.C.

STN. STL. 1"x1/4" BAR GRATING

STN. STL. ANCHOR PLATE FIN. FL.

1/8" 1 1/2"

1/8" 1 1/2"

AS REQUIRED

AS REQUIRED

FLOOR DRAIN BY PLUMBING CONTRACTOR

6" DEEP DEPRESSION

6"

GROUT PAN IN PLACE

DETAIL - FLOOR TROUGH

TYPICAL MECHANICAL SCHEMATIC DISPOSER INSTALLATION

- VACUUM BREAKER BY FSEC
- SPLASH
- COUNTER
- DISPOSER CONE BY FSEC
- ½" CW BY P.C.
- 2" DRAIN BY P.C.
- ½" CW INLET BY P.C.
- FLOW CONTROLS BY P.C.
- 1½" TAILPIECE BY P.C.
- DISPOSER BY FSEC
- GATE VALVE BY P.C.
- SOLENOID VALVE BY FSEC
- GATE VALVE BY P.C.
- CW SUPPLY BY P.C.
- SHOCK STOP BY P.C.
- TIME DELAY RELAY BY FSEC
- MAGNETIC STARTER BY FSEC
- POWER SUPPLY BY E.C.
- DISCONNECT SWITCH BY E.C.

74

12

Sizing a Grease Trap

Single Fixture Installations

STEP 1

Cubic content of a fixture = length × width × depth.

Example: A 3-compartment scullery sink has an overall measurement of 56" × 27". Each compartment is 18" × 24" × 12" = 5,184 cubic inch area; 3 × 5,184 = 15,552 total cubic inch area for 3 compartments.

STEP 2

Content in cubic inches divided by 231 = capacity in U.S. gallons.

Example: $\dfrac{15,552}{231} = 67$ U.S. gal.

STEP 3

Since experience shows that a sink or fixture is seldom filled to the brim and the dishes, pots, or pans displace approximately 25% of the water, we suggest 75% of the actual fixture capacity to be used as a basis to establish the drainage load.

Example: 75% of 67 U.S. gal. = approximately 50 U.S. gal. drainage load.

Step 4

The most generally accepted drainage period is one minute. Conditions may exist (on any given project) however, whereby a longer drainage period could be considered. Therefore, flow rates for this example would be:

$$\frac{\text{Drainage load in gallons}}{\text{Drainage load in minutes}} = \text{Flow rate in GPM}$$

Therefore, flow rates for this example would be:

    50 GPM for 1 minute total drainage
    25 GPM for 2 minute total drainage (should a longer period be desired)

CAUTION: This chart provides basic information only. Check with local health department codes in your area for proper sizing.

Typical Grease Trap Chart

Rating (GPM)	Grease Capacity (lb.)	Length	Width	Height
4	8	17⅛"	9¾"	10"
7	14	19¼"	12⅛"	11⅛"
10	20	23"	14⅛"	11¾"
15	30	25"	16⅞"	13⅜"
20	40	27⅞"	17⅜"	15"
25	50	29⅞"	20"	17"
35	70	31¾"	22⅝"	18¾"
50	100	33⅝"	24⅝"	21½"

13

Plumbing and Electric Data and Conversions

Gas

PIPE SIZING TABLE—MAXIMUM CAPACITY OF PIPE IN CUBIC FEET OF GAS PER HOUR

This table is based on a pressure drop of 0.3 inch water column and 0.6 specific gravity gas.

NOMINAL IRON PIPE SIZE	INTERNAL DIAMETER	\multicolumn{10}{c}{LENGTH OF PIPE}
		10'	20'	30'	40'	50'	60'	70'	80'	90'	100'
½"	.622"	132	92	73	63	56	50	46	43	40	38
¾"	.824"	278	190	152	130	115	105	96	90	84	79
1"	1.049"	520	350	285	245	215	195	180	170	160	150
1¼"	1.380"	1050	730	590	500	440	400	370	350	320	305
1½"	1.610"	1600	1100	890	760	670	610	560	530	490	460
2"	2.067"	3050	2100	1650	1450	1270	1150	1050	990	930	870
2½"	2.469"	4800	3300	2700	2300	2000	1850	1700	1600	1500	1400
3"	3.068"	8500	5900	4700	4100	3600	3250	3000	2800	2600	2500
4"	4.026"	17500	12000	9700	8300	7400	6800	6200	5800	5400	5100

Bottled Gas—Natural Gas Comparison

Bottled Gas	Natural Gas
1 cubic foot	2.4 cubic feet
1 decitherm	9.52 cubic feet
1 pound	20.57 cubic feet
1 gallon	87.22 cubic feet
1 therm	95.23 cubic feet

One cubic foot natural gas = 1050 Btu

One cubic foot LP gas = 2500 Btu

Btu Values for Bottled Gas

Bottled Gas		Btu Value
one cubic foot	=	2,520 Btu
one decitherm	=	10,000 Btu
one pound	=	21,560 Btu
one gallon	=	91,584 Btu
one therm	=	100,000 Btu

Common Utilities Conversions

Multiply	By	To Find
Btu	100000	therm
therm	.00001	Btu
therm	100	cubic foot (natural gas)
cubic foot (natural gas)	.01	therm
watt	.001	kilowatt
kilowatt	1000	watt
kilowatt hour	1.341	horsepower hour
horsepower hour	.746	kilowatt hour
kilowatt hour	3412	Btu
Btu	.0003	kilowatt hour
horsepower hour	2545	Btu
Btu	.0004	horsepower hour
cubic foot (liquid)	7.48	gallon
gallon	.134	cubic foot (liquid)
gallon (water)	8.33	pounds
pounds	.12	gallon

AMPERAGE SIZING GUIDE - KILOWATTS

KILO-WATTS K.W.'S	AMPERAGE SINGLE PHASE 1φ - (60 HERTZ)			AMPERAGE THREE PHASE 3φ - (60 HERTZ)		
	110/1φ & 125/1φ	120/208/1φ & 208/1φ	120/250/1φ & 250/1φ	120/208/3φ & 208/3φ	120/250/3φ & 250/3φ	440/3φ TO 480/3φ
.05	.42	.24	.21	.14	.12	.06
.1	.84	.48	.42	.28	.24	.12
.2	1.7	.96	.84	.56	.49	.24
.3	2.5	1.5	1.3	.83	.73	.36
.4	3.4	1.9	1.7	1.1	.97	.48
.5	4.2	2.4	2.1	1.4	1.2	.60
.6	5.0	2.9	2.5	1.7	1.5	.72
.7	5.9	3.4	2.9	2.0	1.7	.84
.8	6.7	3.9	3.4	2.2	2.0	.96
.9	7.5	4.3	3.8	2.5	2.2	1.1
1.0	8.4	4.8	4.2	2.8	2.4	1.2
2.0	16.7	9.6	8.4	5.6	4.9	2.4
3.0	25.0	14.4	12.5	8.3	7.3	3.6
4.0	33.4	19.3	16.7	11.1	9.7	4.8
5.0	41.7	24.1	20.9	13.9	12.1	6.0
6.0	50.0	28.9	25.0	16.7	14.6	7.2
7.0	58.4	33.7	29.2	19.4	17.0	8.5
8.0	66.7	38.5	33.4	22.2	19.4	9.6
9.0	75.0	43.3	37.5	25.0	21.8	10.8
10.0	83.4	48.1	41.7	27.8	24.3	12.0
20.0	166.7	96.2	83.4	55.5	48.5	24.1
30.0	250.0	144.3	125.0	83.3	72.7	36.1
40.0	333.4	192.3	166.7	111.0	96.9	48.1
50.0	416.7	240.4	208.4	138.8	121.2	60.2
60.0	500.0	288.5	250.0	166.6	145.4	72.2
70.0	583.4	336.6	291.7	194.3	169.6	84.2
80.0	666.7	384.6	333.4	222.1	193.9	96.2
90.0	750.0	432.7	375.0	249.8	218.1	108.3
100.0	833.4	480.8	416.7	277.6	242.3	120.3

NOTE: One kilowatt = 1000 watts. Therefore, to convert watts into kilowatts move decimal point of watts to left three places. (3550. watts = 3.550 K.W.'s) To find amperage, using the above chart a 208/1φ - 3.550 K.W. Hot Food Pan is:

```
                    3.00 K.W. = 14.40 AMPS
                    0.50 K.W. =  2.40 AMPS
                    0.05 K.W. =   .24 AMPS
```

TOTAL K.W. =   3.55 K.W. or 17.04 AMPS

AMPERAGE SIZING GUIDE - HORSEPOWER

HORSE POWER H.P.	AMPERAGE SINGLE PHASE 1φ			AMPERAGE THREE PHASE 3φ		
	110/1φ TO 125/1φ	208/1φ	250/1φ	208/3φ	250/3φ	440/3φ TO 480/3φ
¼	5.8	3.3	2.9	1.1	1.0	.5
1/3	7.2	4.2	3.6	1.4	1.2	.6
½	9.8	5.6	4.9	2.0	1.7	.9
¾	13.8	7.9	6.9	2.9	2.5	1.2
1	16.0	9.2	8.0	4.1	3.6	1.8
1½	20.0	11.5	10.0	5.6	4.9	2.4
2	24.0	13.8	12.0	7.4	6.4	3.2
3	34.0	19.6	17.0	10.8	9.4	4.7
5	56.0	32.2	28.0	16.6	14.4	7.2
7½	†	46.0	40.0	24.7	21.5	10.7
10	†	57.5	50.0	30.8	26.8	13.4
12½	†	†	†	37.9	33.0	16.5
15	†	†	†	45.1	39.2	19.6
20	†	†	†	58.9	51.2	25.6
25	†	†	†	74.5	64.8	32.4
30	†	†	†	86.9	75.6	37.8
40	†	†	†	116.0	101.0	50.4
50	†	†	†	143.0	124.0	62.2

†Not applicable to general kitchen equipment; under voltage and amperage listed. Contact Avtec Factory or Rep. for special order.

CRES-COR CROWN-X

MOBILE FOOD SERVICE AND INSTAMATIC COOKING EQUIPMENT
CRESCENT METAL PRODUCTS INC. 12711 TAFT CLEVELAND OHIO 44108

Electrical Datas	FL-1484-A
Rev. 3 (8/92)	

IMPORTANT ADVICE
BEFORE ORDERING AND USING ELECTRICAL EQUIPMENT

Make sure that your order contains all critical information, and is correctly specified.

Every electrical device shipped from the factory carries a nameplate which specifies the voltage and other characteristics of the device. Be suspicious. Always check the nameplate data before connecting the device. Here's what can happen if you fail to follow this simple procedure:

Wires that are too small will result in improper heating and possible fire hazards.

If you use a 240V device connected to a 120V circuit, you'll lose approximately 75% efficiency.

If you use 240V equipment on 208V lines, you'll lose approximately 25% efficiency, and slow down the pre-heat time as well as recovery of temperature.

If you use 208V equipment on 240V lines, you'll boost the wattage by approximately 25%. This overloaded condition will reduce the life of the heating elements. When in doubt, always consult your electric utility specialist and/or electrical contractor before installing new equipment

Here's a final tip: Always secure a recommendation from your utility specialist for the method of metering to obtain best possible electric rates.

Act on the counsel offered above, and you'll have a top-performing, trouble-free kitchen — and you'll save costs, delays, and loss of efficiency.

UL and CSA have set new standards to protect your personnel and to meet the very latest codes. We have incorporated them in our products.

GLOSSARY OF ELECTRICAL TERMS

Ampere — The rate of flow of electricity through a conductor.

BTU — British Thermal Units. In terms of heat, 3,413 BTU's equal one kilowatt hour.

Circuit — A conductor or a system of conductors through which an electric current flows.

Circuit Breaker or Fuse — A load limiting device that automatically interrupts an electric circuit if an overload condition occurs.

Conductor — If a material will permit electric current to flow through it, it is known as a "conductor;" if it will not permit current to flow, it is an "insulator."

Cycle — Frequency of alternating current expressed in hertz. 60 cycles per second = 60 hertz.

Kilowatt — One thousand watts. Most commercial kitchen equipment is rated in kilowatts.

Kilowatt Hours — The work done by 1 kw in 1 hour. Kwhrs are recorded by the meter.

Name Plate — A plate — or label — attached to the appliance stating the electrical characteristics of that appliance in volts, watts, amperes, phase, and type of current (AC or DC). It will also usually state the model number and the serial number of the appliance.

Single Phase — A circuit energized by a single alternating voltage.

Three Phase — Three separate sources of alternate current so arranged that the peaks of voltage follow each other in a regular, repeating pattern.

Volt — The push that moves electrical current through a conductor.

Watt — A unit of electrical power. One watt equals the flow of one amp at a pressure of one volt (Watts = Volts X Amps).

WIRING CAPACITY TABLE

MAXIMUM KW LOAD PER CIRCUIT*				AMPERES CAPACITY			
Single Phase or DC		Three Phase Balanced		Fuse	Switch	Circuit Breaker	Size Type RHW or THW Wire (Awg.)
120V	240V	208V	240V				
2.0	2.8	4.2	4.9	15	30	15	12**
NOTE: When	3.8	5.7	6.6	20	30	20	12
Appliance	5.7	8.5	9.9	30	30	30	10
Rating	7.6	11.5	13.3	40	60	40	8
Is More	9.6	14.3	16.6	50	60	50	6
Than	11.5	17.2	19.9	60	60	60	6
2.0 KW,	13.4	20.1	23.2	70	100	70	4
208 or 240	15.3	23.0	26.6	80	100	80	4
Volt	17.2	25.9	29.9	90	100	90	2
Equipment	19.2	28.7	33.2	100	100	100	2
Should Be	21.1	31.6	36.5	110	200	110	2
Recommended.	24.0	35.9	41.5	125	200	125	1
	28.8	43.1	49.8	150	200	150	0

*KW load is based on 80% of circuit capacity. **For commercial work, wire size should not be smaller than No. 12 Awg. For runs longer than 50 feet, use next larger size wire.

Plumbing and Electric Data and Conversions **81**

Electrical Datas	FL-1484-A

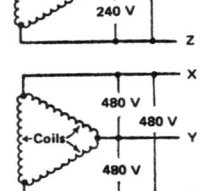

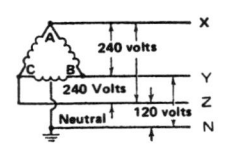

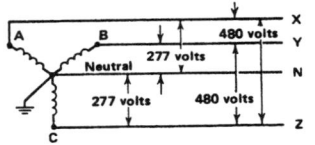

CRES-COR® CROWN-X

MOBILE FOOD SERVICE AND INSTAMATIC COOKING EQUIPMENT
CRESCENT METAL PRODUCTS INC. 12711 TAFT CLEVELAND OHIO 44108

AMPERE FORMULAS

$\frac{W}{V} = A$ Formula for determining Amperes for Single Phase Power Supply:
Watts divided by volts = Amperes:
Example: 200 W ÷ 120 Volts = 1.66 Amperes

Formula for determining Amperes for Three Phase Power Supply:

$\frac{W}{1.73 \times V} = A$ $\frac{Watts}{1.73 \times Volts} =$ Amperes   Example: $\frac{8000}{1.73 \times 230} = 20.1$ Amperes

U.S. VOLTAGE / PHASE COMBINATIONS

1. **120 Volts — Single Phase:**
A two-wire system consisting of one hot and one neutral wire. The voltage between hot and neutral is 125 volts maximum.

2. **240 Volts — Single Phase:**
A two-wire system consisting of two hot wires. The voltage between the two hot wires is 250 Volts maximum.

3. **120-240 Volts — Single Phase:**
(Edison System) A three-wire system consisting of two hot and one neutral wire. The voltage between either hot and neutral is 125 volts maximum and the voltage between the two hot wires is 250 volts maximum.

4. **120/208 Volts — Three Phase:**
A four-wire system consisting of three hot and one neutral wire. Used for three phase power circuits and single phase light and power branch circuits. The voltage between any single hot wire and neutral is 125 Volts maximum. Voltage between any two hot wires is 208 volt single phase. Voltage between three hot wires is 208 volt three phase.

5. **240 Volts — Three Phase:**
A three-wire Delta Connected system consisting of three hot wires. The voltage between any two hot wires is 240 Volts maximum.

6. **480 Volts — Three Phase:**
A three-wire Delta Connected system consisting of three hot wires. The voltage between any two hot wires is 480 Volts maximum.

7. **120-240 Volts — Three Phase:**
A four wire Delta Connected system with Center Tap consisting of three hot wires and one neutral wire. The voltage between either hot line adjacent to the center tap and neutral is 120 Volts maximum. The voltage between any two hot wires is 240 Volts maximum.

8. **480/277 Volts — Three Phase:**
A four-wire system consisting of three hot wires and one neutral wire. Used for 480 Volt three phase power circuits and 277 Volt single phase lighting circuits. The voltage between any hot wire and neutral wire is 277 volts maximum. The voltage between any two hot wires is 480 Volts single phase and between three hot wires is 480 Volts three phase maximum.

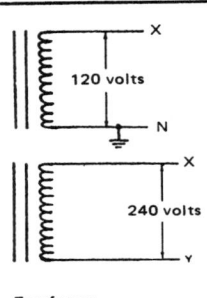

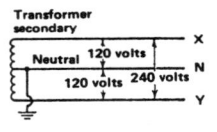

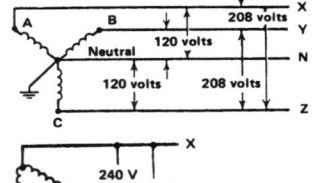

GROUND CONNECTIONS TO ANY OF THE ABOVE SYSTEMS ARE REQUIRED BY CODES.

82 Food Equipment Digest

CRES-COR CROWN-X
MOBILE FOOD SERVICE AND INSTAMATIC COOKING EQUIPMENT
CRESCENT METAL PRODUCTS INC. 12711 TAFT CLEVELAND OHIO 44108

Electrical Data	FL-1484-A

STANDARD PLUGS AND RECEPTACLES

An industry-wide standard has been in effect for a number of years to standardize the configuration of electrical plugs and receptacles. CRES-COR and CROWN-X equipment is made in accordance with these standards.

Illustrated on this sheet are the standard plugs used on CRES-COR and CROWN-X equipment. Illustrated next to the plugs are the required receptacle configurations. These are shown to serve as a guide.

If you receive CRES-COR or CROWN-X equipment which will not fit into your existing receptacles, then both the receptacle and the supply wiring should be checked by an electrician and changed as required.

VOLTAGE	STD. CORD SIZES	WATTAGE	SINGLE PHASE NON-LOCKING RECEPTACLE	PLUG	SINGLE PHASE LOCKING RECEPTACLE	PLUG
120 VOLTS 15 AMPS	18/3 16/3 14/3	USED WITH UNITS OF 1500W OR LESS	 5-15R	 5-15P	 L5-15R	 L5-15P
120 VOLTS 20 AMPS	12/3	USED WITH UNITS OF 1500-2000 WATTS	 5-20R	 5-20P	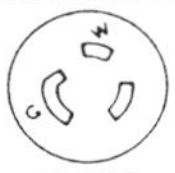 L5-20R	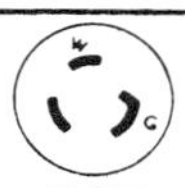 L5-20P
120 VOLTS 30 AMPS	10/3	USED WITH UNITS OF 2000-3000 WATTS	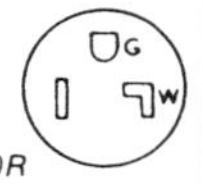 5-30R	 5-30P	 L5-30R	 L5-30P
120 VOLTS 50 AMPS	6/3	USED WITH UNITS OF 3000-5000 WATTS	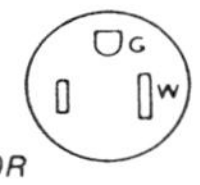 5-50R	 5-50P	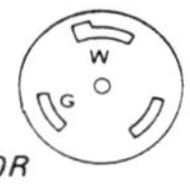 L5-50R	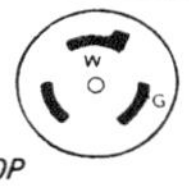 L5-50P
208, 240 VOLTS 15 AMPS	18/3 16/3 14/3	USED WITH UNITS OF 3000W OR LESS	 6-15R	 6-15P	 L6-15R	 L6-15P
208, 240 VOLTS 20 AMPS	12/3	USED WITH UNITS OF 3000-4000 WATTS	 6-20R	 6-20P	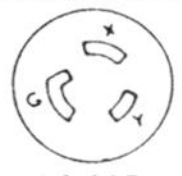 L6-20R	 L6-20P
208, 240 VOLTS 30 AMPS	10/3	USED WITH UNITS OF 4000-6000 WATTS	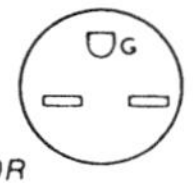 6-30R	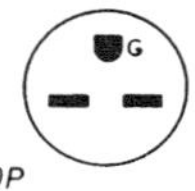 6-30P	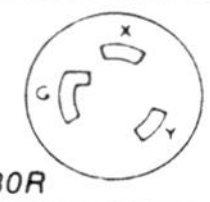 L6-30R	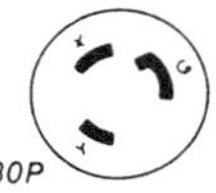 L6-30P
208, 240 VOLTS 50 AMPS	6/3	USED WITH UNITS OF 6000-10,000 WATTS	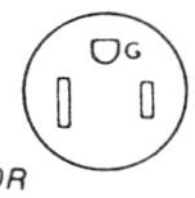 6-50R	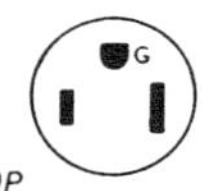 6-50P		

Approximate diameter of power supply cords used on CRES-COR and CROWN-X Equipment. Two wire conductors with ground wire. Diameters shown in inches.

CORD SIZES:	18/3	16/3	14/3	12/3	10/3	6/3
diam.	.330	.360	.395	.630	.690	1.010

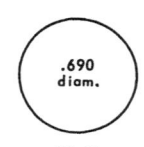

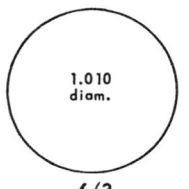

Plumbing and Electric Data and Conversions **83**

Electrical Datas	FL-1484-A

CRES-COR
CROWN-X

MOBILE FOOD SERVICE AND INSTAMATIC COOKING EQUIPMENT
CRESCENT METAL PRODUCTS INC. 12711 TAFT CLEVELAND OHIO 44108

ENERGY UNIT MEASURE BTU CONVERSION CHART

Convert energy usage to Btu's (British Thermal Unit) to eliminate differences in unit measurement for types of fuel.

Electricity: kilowatt hours (kwh) x 3413
Natural gas: cubic feet x 1000
Kerosene: gallons x 134,000
Butane: gallons x 103,300
Propane: gallons x 91,600
Steam: pounds x 1000
Coal: pounds x 13,000
Wood: pounds x 8,800
#2 oil: gallons x 138,200
#4 oil: gallons x 144,000
#5 oil: gallons x 150,000
#6 oil: gallons x 152,000

Convert to million Btu's by dividing figures by 1,000,000 OR to therms by dividing figures by 100,000.

ELECTRICAL POWER REQUIREMENT CHART

The following tables are included to aid you in determining the power requirement for your Cres-Cor and Crown-X equipment.

By locating the proper voltage and wattage on the chart, the current consumption of the equipment can be determined. The current consumption shown in the chart is in Amperes.

WATTS

VOLTS	500	1000	1500	2000	2500	3000	3500	4000	4500	5000
120 Single Phase	4.2	8.3	12.5	16.7	20.8					
208 Single Phase	2.4	4.8	7.2	9.6	12.0	14.4	16.8	19.2	21.6	24.0
240 Single Phase	2.1	4.2	6.3	8.3	10.4	12.5	14.6	16.7	18.8	20.8
208 3-Phase	1.4	2.8	4.2	5.6	6.9	8.3	9.7	11.1	12.5	13.9
240 3-Phase	1.2	2.4	3.6	4.8	6.0	7.2	8.4	9.6	10.8	12.0
480 3-Phase	.6	1.2	1.8	2.4	3.0	3.6	4.2	4.8	5.4	6.0

WATTS

VOLTS	5500	6000	6500	7000	7500	8000	8500	9000	9500	10000
120 Single Phase										
208 Single Phase	26.4	28.8	31.3	33.7	36.1	38.5	40.9	43.3	45.7	48.1
240 Single Phase	22.9	25.0	27.1	29.2	31.3	33.3	35.4	37.5	39.6	41.7
208 3-Phase	15.3	16.7	18.1	19.5	20.8	22.2	23.6	25.0	26.4	27.8
240 3-Phase	13.2	14.5	15.7	16.9	18.1	19.3	20.5	21.7	22.9	24.1
480 3-Phase	6.6	7.2	7.8	8.4	9.0	9.6	10.2	10.8	11.4	12.0

Litho in U.S.A.

MOTORS electric

AMPERE RATINGS FOR MOTORS

The tables on these pages represent an average for the full-load motor currents listed and are to be used for estimating purposes only.

Motor Rating Horsepower 1 Ø	Speed RPM	Current in Amperes 115 Volts	Current in Amperes 230 Volts*
1/8	3600	2.5	1.2
	1800	2.8	1.4
	1200	3.4	1.7
	900	4.0	2.0
1/6	3600	2.8	1.4
	1800	3.2	1.6
	1200	3.8	1.9
	900	4.5	2.2
1/4	3600	4.0	2.0
	1800	4.6	2.3
	1200	6.1	3.0
	900	7.5	3.7
1/3	3600	4.7	2.3
	1800	5.2	2.6
	1200	6.2	3.1
	900	7.3	3.6
1/2	3600	6.5	3.2
	1800	7.4	3.7
	1200	9.1	4.5
	900	12.8	6.4
3/4	3600	9.0	4.5
	1800	10.2	5.1
	1200	12.5	6.2
	900	15.1	7.5
1	3600	11.7	5.8
	1800	13.0	6.5
	1200	15.1	7.5
	900	15.9	7.9
1-1/2	3600	17.8	8.9
	1800	18.4	9.2
	1200	20.9	10.4
	900	24.9	12.4
2	3600	23.0	11.5
	1800	24.0	12.0
	1200	26.4	13.2
	900	30.0	15.0
3	3600	32	16
	1800	34	17
	1200	36	18
	900	41	20
5	3600	54	27
	1800	56	28
	1200	60	30
	900	66	33
7-1/2	3600	79	39
	1800	80	40
	1200	84	42
	900	98	49
10	3600	97	48
	1800	100	50
	1200	105	52
	900	114	57

*To obtain full-load currents of 208- and 200-volt motors, increase corresponding 230-volt motor currents by 10 and 15 per cent, respectively.

Motor Rating Horsepower 3 Ø	Syn. Speed RPM	110 Volts	220 Volts	440 Volts	550 Volts
1/4	1800	1.9	1.0	0.5	0.4
	1200	2.3	1.2	0.6	0.5
	900	2.9	1.5	0.7	0.6
1/3	1800	2.3	1.2	0.6	0.5
	1200	2.9	1.4	0.7	0.6
	900	3.5	1.8	0.9	0.7
1/2	1200	4.1	2.1	1.0	0.8
	900	5.8	2.9	1.5	1.2
3/4	1800	4.7	2.3	1.2	0.9
	1200	5.7	2.9	1.4	1.1
	900	6.9	3.5	1.7	1.4
1	3600	5.5	2.8	1.4	1.1
	1800	6.1	3.1	1.5	1.2
	1200	7.1	3.5	1.8	1.4
	900	7.5	3.7	1.9	1.5
1-1/2	3600	8.3	4.2	2.1	1.7
	1800	8.6	4.3	2.1	1.7
	1200	9.7	4.9	2.4	1.9
	900	11.6	5.8	2.9	2.3
2	3600	11.1	5.6	2.8	2.2
	1800	11.5	5.8	2.9	2.3
	1200	12.7	6.4	3.2	2.5
	900	14.4	7.2	3.6	2.9
3	3600	15.7	7.9	3.9	3.1
	1800	16.6	8.3	4.1	3.3
	1200	17.8	8.9	4.5	3.6
	900	20.4	10.2	5.1	4.1
5	3600	25.4	12.7	6.3	5.1
	1800	26.4	13.2	6.6	5.3
	1200	28.2	14.1	7.1	5.6
	900	31.2	15.6	7.8	6.2
7-1/2	3600	38.4	19.2	9.6	7.7
	1800	38.6	19.3	9.7	7.7
	1200	40.6	20.3	10.2	8.1
	900	47.6	23.8	11.9	9.5
10	3600	49.0	24.5	12.3	9.8
	1800	50.4	25.2	12.6	10.1
	1200	53.2	26.6	13.3	10.6
	900	57.8	28.9	14.5	11.6
	600	67.6	33.8	16.9	13.5
15	3600	73.4	36.7	18.4	14.7
	1800	76.2	38.1	19.1	15.2
	1200	79.8	39.9	20.0	16.0
	900	83.8	41.9	21.0	16.8
	600	96.6	48.3	24.2	19.3
20	3600	98	49.0	24.5	19.6
	1800	101	50.5	25.3	20.2
	1200	103	51.7	25.9	20.6
	900	109	54.6	27.3	21.8
	600	123	61.5	30.8	24.6
25	3600	118	59.2	29.6	23.6
	1800	125	62.7	31.3	25.0
	1200	129	64.7	32.3	25.8
	900	135	67.4	33.7	27.0
	600	144	71.9	35.9	28.8
30	1800	146	72.8	36.4	29.2
	1200	154	77.1	38.6	30.8
	900	159	79.4	39.7	31.8
	600	176	87.9	43.9	35.2

Motor Rating Horsepower 3 Ø	Syn. Speed RPM	110 Volts	220 Volts	440 Volts	550 Volts
40	1800	196	98	49.0	39.2
	1200	198	99	49.5	39.6
	900	208	104	52.0	41.6
	600	226	113	56.5	45.2
50	1800	242	121	60.5	48.4
	1200	244	122	61.0	48.8
	900	254	127	63.5	50.8
	600	276	138	69.0	55.2
60	1800	......	143	71.5	57.2
	1200	......	148	74.0	59.2
	900	......	151	75.5	60.4
	600	......	162	81.0	64.8
75	1800	......	178	89.0	71.2
	1200	......	181	90.5	72.4
	900	......	187	93.5	74.8
	600	......	199	99.5	79.6
100	1800	......	233	116	93.2
	1200	......	239	120	95.6
	900	......	245	123	98.0
	600	......	257	128	103
	450	......	290	145	116
125	1800	......	289	144	115
	1200	......	298	149	119
	900	......	305	153	122
	720	......	314	157	126
	600	......	320	160	128
	450	......	351	175	140
150	1800	......	346	173	138
	1200	......	350	175	140
	900	......	363	182	145
	720	......	376	188	150
	600	......	378	189	151
	450	......	418	209	166
200	1800	......	460	230	184
	1200	......	466	233	186
	900	......	490	245	196
	720	......	494	247	197
	600	......	498	249	199
	450	......	528	264	211
250	1800	......	572	286	229
	1200	......	580	290	232
	900	......	604	302	242
	720	......	625	312	250
	600	......	630	315	252
	450	......	630	315	252
	360	......	676	338	270
300	1800	......	685	342	274
	1200	......	696	348	278
	900	......	722	361	289
	600	......	722	361	289
	450	......	760	380	304
	360	......	830	415	332
400	1800	......	910	455	364
	1200	......	933	466	373
	600	......	955	477	382
	450	......	1000	500	400
	360	......	1050	523	418
500	1800	......	1160	578	462
	1200	......	1120	560	448
	600	......	1180	590	472
	450	......	1200	602	482
	360	......	1320	658	526

Electrical Ratings

Watts	Volts	Phase	Amps	Breaker or Fuse Size
4 kW	208	1	19	30
	240	1	17	30
	480	1	8	15
5 kW	208	1	24	30
	240	1	21	30
	480	1	10	15
6 kW	208	1	29	40
	208	3	25*	40
	240	1	25	40
	240	3	22*	30
	480	3	11*	15
	600	3	6	15
7 kW	208	1	34	50
	208	3	29*	40
	240	1	29	40
	240	3	25*	40
	480	3	13*	20
	600	3	7	15
9 kW	208	1	43	60
	208	3	38*	50
	240	1	38	50
	240	3	33*	50
	480	3	16*	20
	600	3	9	15
9.9 kW	208	1	47.5	60
	208	3 (BAL.)	27.5	40
10.4 kW	208	3 (BAL.)	28.8	40
11.4 kW	240	1	47.5	60
	240	3 (BAL.)	27.5	40
	480	3 (BAL.)	13.7	20
12 kW	208	1	58	90
	208	3	33	50
	240	1	50	70
	240	3	29	40

Watts	Volts	Phase	Amps	Breaker or Fuse Size
12 kW *(continued)*				
	480	3	14	20
	600	3	12	20
13.5 kW	208	1	65	90
	208	3	38	50
	240	1	56	70
	240	3	33	50
	480	3	16	20
	600	3	13	20
15 kW	208	1	72	90
	208	3	42	60
	240	1	63	90
	240	3	36	50
	480	3	18	30
	600	3	15	20
17.25 kW	208	3	48	60
18 kW	208	1	86	125
	240	1	75	100
	240	3	43	60
	480	3	21	30
	600	3	18	30
24 kW	208	1	115	150
	208	3	67	90
	240	1	100	125
	240	3	58	90
	480	3	29	40
	600	3	24	30
27 kW	208	1	130	175
	208	3	75	100
	240	1	113	150
	240	3	65	90
	480	3	33	50
	600	3	26	40
30 kW	208	1	144	200
	208	3	83	125
	240	1	125	175

Plumbing and Electric Data and Conversions

Watts	Volts	Phase	Amps	Breaker or Fuse Size
30 kW *(continued)*				
	240	3	72	90
	480	3	36	50
	600	3	29	40
36 kW	208	1	173	225
	208	3	100	125
	240	1	150	200
	240	3	87	125
	480	3	43	60
	600	3	35	50
39 kW	208	1	188	250
	208	3	108	150
	240	1	163	225
	240	3	94	125
	480	3	47	60
	600	3	38	50
40.5 kW	208	3	112	150
	240	3	97	125
	480	3	49	60
	600	3	40	50
45 kW	208	3	125	175
	240	1	188	250
	240	3	108	150
	480	3	54	70
	600	3	44	60
54 kW	208	3	150	200
	240	3	130	175
	480	3	65	90
	600	3	52	70
58.5 kW	208	3	161	225
	240	3	141	200
	480	3	71	90
	600	3	57	90

*Open Delta (unbalanced load) amperage of high leg indicated.

14

Stainless Steel Fabrication

Stainless Steel Thickness and Weight

Gauge	Thickness	Decimal	Weight (per sq. ft.)	Weight (4N × 10N sheet)
12	7/64"	.1046	4.375 lb.	175.00 lb.
14	5/64"	.0747	3.125 lb.	125.00 lb.
16	1/16"	.0598	2.500 lb.	100.00 lb.
18	3/64"	.0478	2.000 lb.	80.00 lb.
20	1/32"	.0359	1.500 lb.	60.00 lb.
22	3/128"	.0299	1.250 lb.	50.00 lb.

Typical Gauges for Stainless Steel Fabrication

Item	Gauge
Sink bowls	12, 14, 16, 18
Drainboards	12, 14, 16
Worktables	12, 14, 16
Undershelves	12, 14, 16
Wall shelving	16, 18, 20
Counter (tops)	12, 14, 16, 18
Single pan doors	18
Double pan doors	18, 20

89

Item	Gauge
Side panels	16, 18, 20
Back panels	18, 20, 22
Interior shelves	16, 18
Exhaust hoods	18, 20
Exhaust ductwork	16, 18
Wall protection	12, 14, 16
Kick plates	16

15

Flatware: Suggested Requirements

Flatware: General Operations

Item	Amount in Service × Seats	Reserve × Seats
Knives	2–3	2
Dinner forks	4	4
Teaspoons	1½–2	2
Soup spoons	1½	1½
Salad forks	½	½
Ice drink spoons	½	½

Figures represent requirements per seat.

Flatware: Specific Operations

Item	Hotel (Formal)	Restaurant
Teaspoons	5	4
Dessert/soup spoons	2	2
Tablespoons	¼	¼
Ice drink spoons	¾	¾
A.D. coffee spoons	2	¼
Bouillion spoons	2	2
Dinner forks	3	3

Item	Hotel (Formal)	Restaurant
Salad/dessert forks	1	1
Oyster cocktail forks	½	½
Knives	2	2

Glassware: Suggested Requirements

Item	Capacity	Bar/Lounge	Restaurant	Cater
Beer	7–12 oz.	12 dz.	12 dz.	12 dz.
Champagne	4½–6 oz.	3 dz.	3 dz.	12 dz.
Cocktail	3–5 oz.	9 dz.	6 dz.	12 dz.
High Ball	7–11 oz.	12 dz.	9 dz.	12 dz.
Wines	6½–9 oz.	6 dz.	9 dz.	9 dz.
Sours	5–6 oz.	3 dz.	3 dz.	—
Rocks	4–7 oz.	9 dz.	6 dz.	9–12 dz.
Cordials	¾–1½ oz.	3 dz.	3 dz.	—
Collins	9–12 oz.	3 dz.	3 dz.	—
Brandy	2–20 oz.	3 dz.	3 dz.	—

Steamtable Pan: Approximate Number of Servings per Pan

Full Size, 20¾" × 12¾"

Depth (in.)	Volume (qt.)	1 oz.	2 oz.	4 oz.	8 oz.
1¼	Deli Pan				
2½	8.3	268	134	67	33
4	14	424	212	106	53
6	21	644	322	161	80

Two-thirds Size, 13⅞" × 12¾"

Depth (in.)	Volume (qt.)	1 oz.	2 oz.	4 oz.	8 oz.
2½	5½	176	88	44	22
4	9.3	296	148	74	37
6	14	452	226	113	56

Half Size, 10⅜" × 12¾"

Depth (in.)	Volume (qt.)	1 oz.	2 oz.	4 oz.	8 oz.
1¼	Deli Pan				
2½	4.3	128	64	32	16
4	7	214	107	53	27
6	10	322	161	80	40

Flatware: Suggested Requirements

Half Size Long, 20¾" × 6⁷⁄₁₆"

Depth (in.)	Volume (qt.)	1 oz.	2 oz.	4 oz.	8 oz.
2½	4	120	60	30	15
4	6	184	92	46	23
6	8	264	132	66	33

One-third Size, 6⁷⁄₈" × 12¾"

Depth (in.)	Volume (qt.)	1 oz.	2 oz.	4 oz.
2½	2½	85	42	21
4	4	134	67	33
6	6	197	98	49

One-fourth Size, 6⅜" × 10⅜"

Depth (in.)	Volume (qt.)	1 oz.	2 oz.	4 oz.
2½	2	60	30	15
4	3	96	48	24
6	4½	146	73	36

One-sixth Size, 6⁷⁄₈" × 6¼"

Depth (in.)	Volume (qt.)	1 oz.	2 oz.
2½	1	40	20
4	2	60	30
6	3	87	43

One-ninth Size, 6⁷⁄₈" × 4¼"

Depth (in.)	Volume (qt.)	1 oz.	2 oz.
2	½	8	6
4	1	18	13

Utensils: Scoop and Ladle Equivalents

Scoop Size	Measurement Equivalent	Per Gallon
No. 6	⅔ cup	16
No. 8	½ cup	22
No. 10	⅝ cup	24
No. 12	⅓ cup	26
No. 16	¼ cup	35
No. 20	3+ tbsp	42

Scoop Size	Measurement Equivalent	Per Gallon
No. 24	2⅔ tbsp	51
No. 30	2+ tbsp	62
No. 40	1½ tbsp	70

Soup/Sauce Ladles

Size	Equivalent
1 oz.	⅛ cup
2 oz.	¼ cup
4 oz.	½ cup
6 oz.	¾ cup
8 oz.	1 cup

Utensils: Suggested Guide for Utensil Selection in Kitchen

To feed 100 people.

Item	Quantity
Egg beater	1
Measuring spoons	1 set
Oven/freezer mitt	2 pair
Brushes, flat & round	4
Rolling pin	1
Whip (10", 12", 16", 18")	4
Covers/stands	2
Display cases	1
Pie makers	1
Bread pans	12
Sheet pans/cake (assorted sizes)	6–12
Jello molds (individual or large molds)	36 or 3
Muffin tins (24 count)	6
Pie tins	12
Dredges	2
Funnels	3
Measures (1, 2, 4 qt.)	3
Coffee maker	1–2
Coffee decanters	6–12
Silver compartment (storage boxes)	3

Flatware: Suggested Requirements

Item	Quantity
Sauce pans (1½, 2¾, 3¾, 5½, 7, 10 qt.)	6
Sauce pots (14, 26 qts)	2
Stock pots (3, 6, 10 gal.)	3
Double boiler (8, 12 qt.)	2
Bake pans	6
Roast pans	2
China caps (9")	1
Clam/oyster knives	6
Colander	1
Strainer (6", 8", 10", 12")	4
Hot food service (Pan 2000 series, full, ½, ⅓, ¼, ⅙)	24
Covers for pans	12
Skimmers (4½", 6")	2
Frypans (8", 10", 12", 14")	6
Butter spreaders	1
Egg poacher	1
Steak weight	1
Thermometers:	
deep fat	1
oven	1
pocket	1
roast	1
Basting spoon (solid, perforated, slotted)	6
Ladles (one 24 oz.)	6
Paddles (30–48)	1
Tongs (6", 9", 12")	6
Turner	2
Can opener (#1 or #2)	1
Cheese cutter	1
Egg slicer	2
Food mill	1
Tomato tamer	1
Baker's scraper	1
Oven brush/scraper	2
Pastry bags	6
Pastry tips	6
Scrapers	2

Item	Quantity
Food storage boxes	6
Ingredient bins	3
Mixing bowls	12
Scale portion control	1
Scale, bakery	1
Scoops (24, 32, 48 oz.)	3
Utility dish pans	2
Storage containers	12
Coffee tank (3.5 gal.)	1
Multipurpose rubber matting (26 × 50")	1
Safety-mats	3–6
Ice cream scoops (various sizes)	6
Juice dispenser	1–2
Juice extractor	1
Boning knives	2
Cleaver	1
Paring knives	6
Pot forks	2
Slicers	4–6
Spatulas	2
Box grater	1
Broiler scraper	1
Carton opener	1
Lobster crackers	24
Parers & corers	6
Poultry shears	6
Sharpening stones	1
Storage containers (2–22 qt)	10–12
Chopping bowls	1
Cutting boards	2
Dish cloths	24
Towels, linen	36
S/S pails	1–2
Liquid grill cleaner	1 gal.
S/S cleaner	1 case
Aluminum foil (several sizes)	3
Grill bricks	12

Flatware: Suggested Requirements

Item	Quantity
Neoprene gloves	6 pair
Plastic aprons	6
Plastic garbage bags	1 unit
Scouring pads	12
Floor squeegee	1
Mops/heads	6
Brooms	2
Mop wringer/pail	1
Pick-up brush/pail	1
Vacuum cleaner	1
Storage container (flour, sugar, etc.)	3
Waste receptacles (various sizes)	6–12
Glass washing brush	1
Urn brush	1

Food Trade Magazines and Associations

Food Trade Magazines

Food Distributors Magazine
P.O. Box 10378
Clearwater, Fl 34617

Food Management Magazine
747 Third Avenue
New York, NY 10017

Foodservice Distributor
1100 Superior Avenue
Cleveland, Oh 44114

Foodservice Equipment & Supplies Specialist
1350 East Touhy Avenue
Des Plaines, IL 60017

Nation's Restaurant News
524 Park Avenue
New York, NY 10022

Restaurants & Institutions
1350 East Touhy Avenue
Des Plaines, IL 60018

Restaurant Business
633 Third Avenue
New York, NY 10017

Restaurant Hospitality
1100 Superior Avenue
Cleveland, Oh 44114

National Foodservice Associations

American Dietetic Association
216 W. Jackson, Suite 800
Chicago, IL 60606
312-899-0040

American Gas Association
1515 Wilson Boulevard
Arlington, VA 22209
703-841-8400

American Hotel & Motel Association (AH&MA)
1201 New York Avenue N.W., Suite 600
Washington, D.C. 20005
202-289-3100

American Restaurant China Council, Inc.
P.O. Box 7601
Mclean, VA 22106
703-893-4631

Commercial Food Equipment Service Agencies
60 Revere Drive, Suite 500
Northbrook, IL 60062
312-480-9080

Food Equipment Manufacturers Association (FEMA)
401 N. Michigan Avenue
Chicago, IL 60611
312-644-6610

Foodservice Consultants Society International (FCSI)
304 W. Liberty Street, Suite 201
Louisville, KY 40202
502-583-3783

Foodservice Equipment Distributors Association (FEDA)
332 S. Michigan Avenue
Chicago, IL 60604
312-427-9605

International Foodservice Distributors Association
Division of North American Wholesale Grocers Association
201 Park Washington Court
Falls Church, VA 22046
703-532-9400

International Foodservice Manufacturers Association
180 N. Stetson, Suite 4400
Chicago, IL 60601
312-540-4400

Marketing Agents for the Food Service Industry (MAFSI)
401 N. Michigan Avenue
Chicago, IL 60611
312-644-6610

National Association of Food Equipment Manufacturers (NAFEM)
401 N. Michigan Avenue
Chicago, IL 60611
312-644-6610

National Automatic Merchandising Association
20 N. Wacker Drive, Room 3500
Chicago, IL 60606
312-346-0370

National Restaurant Association (NRA)
1200 17th Street N.W.
Washington, D.C. 20036
202-331-5900

National Sanitation Foundation
3475 Plymouth Road
P.O. Box 130140
Ann Arbor, MI 48113
313-769-8010

Permanent Ware Institute
334 S. Main Street
Cayton, OH 45402
312-263-2070

SEFA
3158 Des Plaines Avenue, Suite 115
Des Plaines, IL 60018
708-699-4070

17
Video Tapes

Many manufacturers now have educational videos available to the trade—check your local representatives for availability.

The following manufacturers have tapes available:

Amco

Bettcher Industry

Cambro

Cleveland

Crescent Metal Products

Crimsco Corp.

Dean/Alco

Frymaster

Hatco

Hobart

Hurrisystem, Inc.

Intermetro

Jackson/Alco

Keating

Lincoln Wearever

The Lowenstein Co.

Lucks Company

Magi Kitchen

Mity Lite Tables

Norlake

Panasonic

Perlick Corp.

Robot Coupe

Rubbermaid

Sparta Brush

Taylor Freeze

Vollrath

Vulcan Hart

Welbilt

Wittco

Additional Resources

MANUFACTURER   ADDRESS   PHONE

Manufacturer	Address	Phone